Micros For Educators

A Fundamental Guide to Mastering Microsoft Teams for Education with Step-by-Step Illustrations for Teachers

Tech Treck

© Tech Treck 2020
All right reserved

This book is copyrighted, and no part of this publication may be reproduced or transmitted through any means, be it mechanical, electronic, internet, or otherwise without the permission of the publisher except in a brief quotation or review of the book. The information in this book is believed to be valid at the date of publication. However, neither the author nor the publisher is legally responsible for any errors or omissions that may be made. The publisher makes no warranty, express or implied, concerning the information contained herein.

Printed on-demand in
United Kingdom, United States, and Canada

ISBN: 9798663274173

Table of Contents

LESSON ONE 1
    INTRODUCTION 1
    WHAT IS MICROSOFT TEAMS? 3
    FEATURES OF MICROSOFT TEAMS 4
    HOW MICROSOFT TEAMS WORKS 6
    BENEFITS OF MICROSOFT TEAMS 7
    MICROSOFT TEAMS VIA OFFICE 365 8
    MICROSOFT TEAMS FOR EDUCATION 9

LESSON TWO 11
    SETTING UP MICROSOFT TEAMS 11
    HOW TO SIGN IN WITH A SCHOOL ACCOUNT 11
    DOWNLOAD TEAMS ON YOUR DEVICES 13
    TEAMS FOR EDUCATION INTERFACE 15
    THE NAVIGATION BAR 15
    THE PROFILE BUTTON 17

LESSON THREE 20
    TEAMS AND CHANNELS FEATURES 20
    CHANNELS IN TEAMS AND HOW THEY FUNCTION 22
    ACTIVITY FEED FOR TEACHERS AND STUDENTS 24
    @MENTIONS 26
    CHATS 26
    TABS 27

LESSON FOUR 28
    PERMISSION AND SECURITY IN TEAMS 28
    RESTRICTIONS ON PRIVATE OR PUBLIC CHANNELS 29
    WHAT ARE PRIVATE CHANNELS? 29
    BREAKOUT GROUPS OR PRIVATE CHANNEL 29
    HOW TO MANAGE PRIVATE CHANNELS. 31
    ADDING MEMBERS TO A PRIVATE CHANNEL 31
    PRIVATE CHANNEL SETTINGS 32
    PRIVATE CHANNEL PEOPLE PANE 33
    PRIVATE CHANNEL FILE MANAGEMENT 34
    STUDENTS, AND GUESTS AND EXTERNAL GUEST 35
    TEAMS MEMBER PERMISSION 35

LESSON FIVE 37
CLASSROOMS AS TEAMS 37
CLASS TEAMS 37
TEAM FOR EDUCATORS WORKGROUP/ PROFESSIONAL LEARNING COMMUNITY 38
TEAM FOR STAFF/ SCHOOL ADMINISTRATION AND DEVELOPMENT 38
HOW TO CREATE A CLASS TEAM 39
HOW TO CHANGE DISPLAY ICON OF A CLASS TEAM 43
HOW TO CHANGE YOUR CLASS NAME 45
ADDING STUDENTS TO YOUR CLASS TEAM 46
USING CODE TO ADD STUDENTS TO A CLASS TEAMS 47
CREATING A CLASS CHANNEL IN TEAMS 49
ADDING TABS IN CHANNELS 52

LESSON SIX 54
DOCUMENT MANAGEMENT 54
UPLOADING FILES TO STUDENTS 54
CREATING OFFICE 365 FILES FORMAT IN TEAMS 55
TRANSFER OR COPY FILES AND FOLDERS 56
COLLABORATING WITH A DOCUMENT IN TEAMS 56
CLASS ASSIGNMENT, CLASS NOTEBOOK, AND FILE SHARING 59
CLASS NOTEBOOK IN TEAMS *59*
RUBRIC IN ASSIGNMENTS *65*
CUSTOMIZE YOUR GRADING CRITERIA FOR RUBRIC *66*

LESSON SEVEN 69
VIDEO CONFERENCING 69
AD-HOC MEETINGS 69
PRIVATE OR GROUP MEETINGS 70
CHANNEL MEETINGS 71
HOW TO INVITE A NON-TEAM MEMBER TO A MEETING 73
SETTING MEETING OPTIONS 74
HOW TO SET A PRESENTER IN A TEAM MEETING 75
JOINING A SCHEDULED MEETING 76
STATING A PRIVATE MEETING 77
TEAMS MEETING CONTROLS 78
TEAMS MEETINGS BOMBING 80
RECORDING YOUR MEETINGS 82
SETTING A CUSTOM BACKGROUND 83
HOW TO BLUR YOUR MICROSOFT TEAMS BACKGROUND 84
TEAMS WHITEBOARD SHARING 84
MICROSOFT WHITEBOARD DRAWING FEATURES 85
HOW TO EXPORT A WHITEBOARD CONTENT 86

HOW TO SHARE WHITEBOARD AND CHAT 87
CLASS MEETING ATTENDANCE 88
HOW TO STOP EMAIL NOTIFICATIONS 89

LESSON EIGHT 90

ADVANCED TIPS AND TRICK 90
HOW TO MANAGE NOTIFICATIONS IN TEAMS 90
NOTIFICATION PRIORITY SET UP 91
DO NOT DISTURB AND *92*
HOW TO ENABLE DARK MODE 92
HOW TO TURN ON DARK THEME ON MOBILE DEVICES 94
HOW TO CHANGE TEAMS LAYOUT 95
HOW TO TRANSLATE LANGUAGES IN TEAMS *95*
HOW TO SET KEYBOARD LANGUAGE *98*
HOW TO DISABLE TEAMS FROM STARTING AUTOMATICALLY AND RUNNING IN THE BACKGROUND WHEN CLOSED ON DESKTOPS *98*
HOW TO BLOCK CALLS WITH NO CALLER ID *99*
HOW TO FILTER YOUR ACTIVITY FEEDS *100*
EMAILS MESSAGE TO CHANNELS *102*
MICROSOFT TEAMS KEYBOARD SHORTCUTS *103*
HOW TO SIGN OUT OF TEAMS 105

LESSON ONE

INTRODUCTION

If you are moving your classroom online, then you are in for a lot of exciting changes. The good news is that you can translate learning sessions into a dynamic online environment, which can make your interaction more versatile, collaborative, and reachable.

The global pandemic has made it necessary for schools and students to adopt emergency remote teaching, which has also placed a spotlight on the digital divide in our society.

For schools to improve their educational outcomes from students, adequate provision has to be made to ensure everyone has access to the internet. However, more people that didn't have internet access now have greater access than they did before.

As teachers all over the world are taking a more infused consolidative approach to technology in their classrooms to improve educational outcomes for their students, Microsoft Teams is a big thing in any academic collaboration that schools and teachers should embrace.

The modern learning platform is a different setting than it was in the past. This is due to the growing ability of educators to teach remotely. With an increase in a remote learning environment away from a typical classroom setting, the teacher's job evolves. Several studies show that on the whole, teachers and students who collaborate remotely are more productive than their classroom-bound colleagues, and more pleased with their learning speed as well.

WHAT IS MICROSOFT TEAMS?

Microsoft Teams is an online collaboration and chat cloud app that is designed as a hub for teamwork. It allows you to bring together a team and resources, communicate through chat and messaging. You can also make calls and hold meetings and share or edit documents.

Microsoft Teams integrates with an existing Microsoft 365 business subscription and also features extensions that can integrate with products that are not from Microsoft.

What sets Microsoft Teams apart from its rivals is its all-in-one integration of applications that business users count on, including messaging, Office 365, video meetings, file sharing, collaborative editing, and team-based planning. Microsoft Teams integrates a range of Office 365 capabilities including:
- SharePoint
- Word
- Excel
- PowerPoint
- Power BI
- Planner

FEATURES OF MICROSOFT TEAMS

Microsoft Teams is designed to meet the vital communication and collaboration needs of a modern classroom, regardless of location or type of device.
Key features include:

1. **For Instant messaging**
   - Minimize email sizes between team members
   - Allow team members to work more flexibly
   - Easy-to-read conversation windows with a comprehensive chat history visible
   - Group chat-based messaging with user access controls
   - Connect instantly with team members across locations and devices
   - Receive and customize alerts for chat-based messages
   - Seamless toggling between chat, video calls, voice calls, and screen sharing
   - Private one-on-one chat-based messaging

- Access GIFs, stickers and emojis to support team culture and communication

2. **For Voice and video calls**
   - Call people anywhere in the world and from any device
   - Start a voice or video calls with a single click
   - Make high-quality voice calls and video calls to individuals or groups
   - Use screen-sharing to collaborate in real-time from any location

3. **Meetings**
   - Provide a high-quality interactive video experience for up to 10,000 participants\
   - Easy access to documents and data stored within Office 365
   - Host meetings, presentations and events for users anywhere in the world
   - Record meetings and calls so no-one misses out

4. **Accessibility**
   - Enjoy a seamless user experience, with Teams versions optimized for different devices
   - Switch between devices without hassles or delays
   - Experience high-quality video and audio from any device
   - Work flexibly by accessing Teams on the device that suits – phone, tablet or laptop
   - View, edit and collaborate on documents in real-time from any device

5. **Apps and integrations**
   - Access to add-ons such as Twitter, Trello, Google Analytics and more so teams can access tools they need outside of Office 365 in one place

- Build your custom application, like QBot, for your team or organization
- Integration of Office 365 capabilities in a single workspace including chat, voice, and video calls, file sharing, collaboration, and planning.

6. **Security and compliance**
    - inbuilt security, compliance, and management tools to streamline IT security
    - Cutting-edge data protection capabilities
    - Granular access and security controls

HOW MICROSOFT TEAMS WORKS

Teams provide an easy way to create a distinct environment for project teams, business units, staff, and other groups for effective communication and collaboration. By creating a 'team' and assigning users, organizations can create a private group and chat rooms referred to as '*channels'* to strategies, manage, and deliver tasks. Each team can further set up various channels to focus on specific topics and keep the discussion organized.

For example, you can create a team for your Biology Class and use three separate channels for different sets of students. Channels are easy to use as other popular messaging apps. Conversations among team members are grouped in a thread for easy access to an entire group chat, and messages. Teams member who has access to a channel can receive notifications when a message dropped.

Calls and Video chats within as a group can be started with one click from within an individual channel. Changes can automatically be synced to OneDrive or SharePoint to ensure that the latest version is always available and accessible.

BENEFITS OF MICROSOFT TEAMS

If you are serious about rapid productivity gains, improving classroom meetings, and maximizing the gains in your online tutoring, Microsoft Teams is the collaboration platform for you.

Here are the reasons why school administrations should choose Teams:
1. Microsoft Teams seamlessly integrates with Microsoft Office 365 and other third-party apps.
2. All documents and conversations are stored in an easy to access location. Documents can be edited by team members from any location in real-time.
3. Microsoft Teams is mobile-friendly, allowing users to chat, message, and join meetings with their mobile devices.
4. Microsoft Teams is designed to suit your business needs. It comes with in-built suites of apps and bots to boost your productivity.
5. Scheduling and hosting meetings with team members is easy and syncs with Outlook.

MICROSOFT TEAMS VIA OFFICE 365

Microsoft Teams is not available as a stand-alone service, it requires a Microsoft Office 365 subscription. Microsoft Office 365 is an integrated cloud-based apps and services platform designed to help users pursue their passion and grow their businesses. Apps on the Office 365 hub are constantly updated with the latest features and security patches.

The traditional Office package came as software installed on each user's computer, which includes applications such as Excel Word, Powerpoint, and Outlook. Office 365 goes beyond the core traditional applications with the addition of Skype for Business, Yammer, Sharepoint, OneDrive, and Microsoft Teams. Added to the Office 365 applications include a host of improved cloud services such as Power BI, Delve, Sway, Stream Flow, Planner, and forms.

Office 365 is more powerful than the previous version of Microsoft Office Suite. Office 365 Home and Personal account do not include Microsoft Teams among its packages, you can get it with an Office 365 business or enterprise account.

MICROSOFT TEAMS FOR EDUCATION

Educators can create collaborative classrooms, connect in professional learning communities, and communicate with school staff – all from a single experience in Office 365 for Education and is free for all staff, students, and faculty through Office 365 for Education.

Microsoft Teams for Education allows teachers to promote learning in a virtual classroom away from their usual classroom environment. They can easily connect with students, host virtual learning webinars, host Team Meetings with unlimited pupils, and share or store files. Teachers can also work together with pupils on documents simultaneously irrespective of teacher's and student's location.

The Microsoft Teams for Education is fully integrated with the common applications most students are used to; such as PowerPoint, Excel Word, and Teams can be accessed by Desktop, web Phone, or Tablet. With this amount of accessibility, teachers and students alike can use Microsoft Teams for Education at any time of the day remotely.

LESSON TWO

SETTING UP MICROSOFT TEAMS

Setting up Teams on your mobile device is easy and allows you to stay connected with your class from anywhere, at any time. You can download Teams from the Windows Store (Windows Mobile), App Store (Apple iOS) or Google Play (Android). If your school has an Education license at the Office 365 tenant-level the IT department or administrator will have to enable Teams from the Microsoft 365 admin center.

HOW TO SIGN IN WITH A SCHOOL ACCOUNT

Once your school has access to Microsoft Teams, you can: download the desktop application, access Teams through your browser, or download the mobile app.

1. **Sign in to Office**

    Go to: *office.com*, and sign in with your student or teachers' office account.

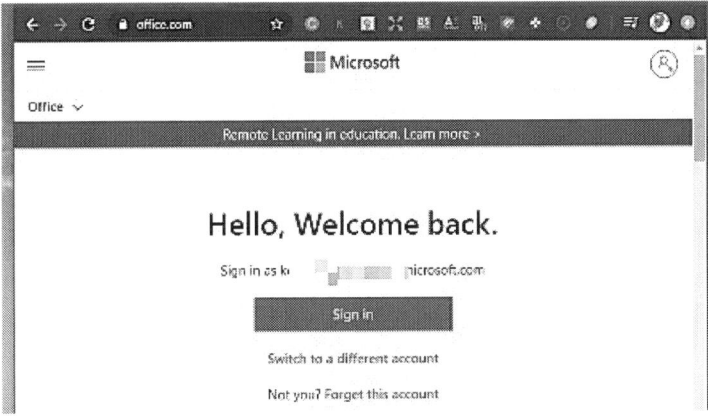

Once you are logged into the Office 365 website, you will see several buttons that allow you to access the Office 365 services. Among these buttons is the Microsoft Teams.

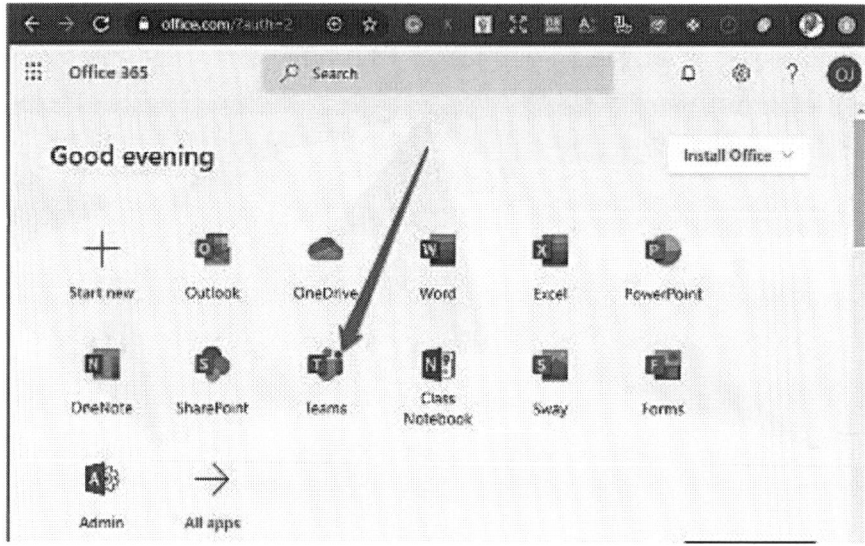

Click on the Microsoft Teams icon in the app portal to get in.

DOWNLOAD TEAMS ON YOUR DEVICES

To download teams on your computer or mobile devices, go to *teams.microsoft.com/downloads* on your browser.

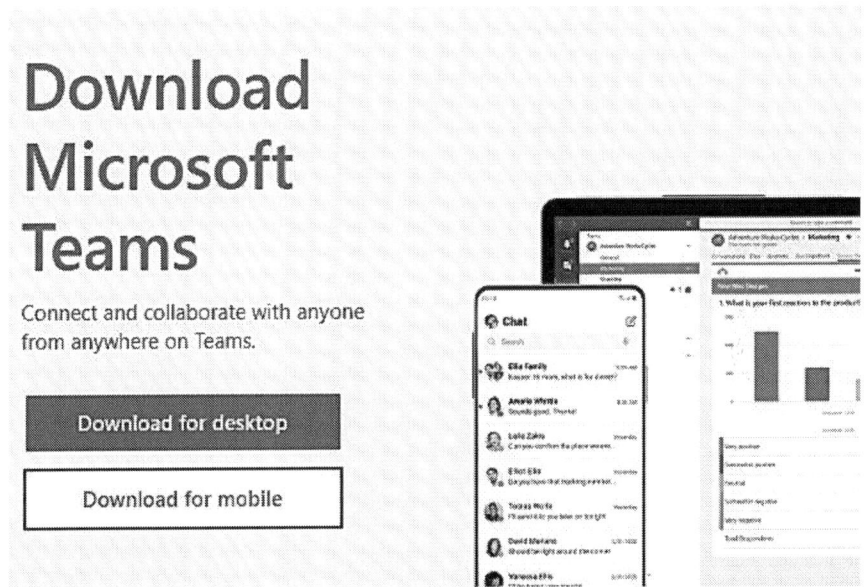

You can download the app on multiple devices (including mobile devices) to stay connected wherever you are.

To sign in to the app on your computer, click on the start button and locate Microsoft teams from the list of apps installed on your computer.

For Mac, go to the Applications folder and select Microsoft Teams.

On your mobile devices, tap on the Teams app icon like you will do with other applications installed on your mobile device.

On the web, use your browser to visit
   teams.microsoft.com

The first time you lunch the app on your device, you will be prompted to enter your school email and password for user authentication. You may have to ask your school admin for your login details.

TEAMS FOR EDUCATION INTERFACE

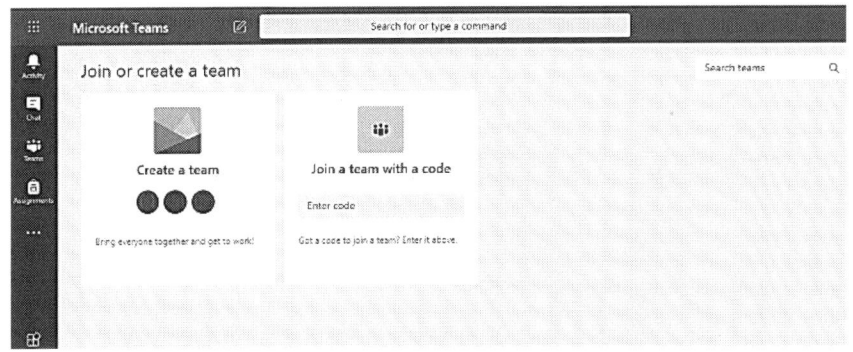

THE NAVIGATION BAR

The Microsoft Teams for Education interface has three basic components. If you are using the web or client based app, on the left of your screen you have the navigation bar with multiple tabs which include: *Activity, Chat, Teams, Assignments, Calendar, Calls, and Files.*

- The **Activity** tab contains activity feeds that contain a summary of everything that has happened in the team and channels you belong to or a summary of your recent activity. To go to the Activity view, press **Ctrl+1**.
- The **Chat** tab is used to carry out text conversation or video calls with students and colleagues.
- The **Teams** tab is used to create classrooms, groups, and channels.
- **Assignment** tab contains features you can use to create assignments, add resources, and grade students.
- **Calender** tab helps you create schedules as well as monitor your schedules.
- **File** tab is used to attached resource materials for your online classroom.

You will also see a three- white dot ellipsis icon that when clicked, pops-up a window with additional apps, like OneNote, Teams Planner, and Help.

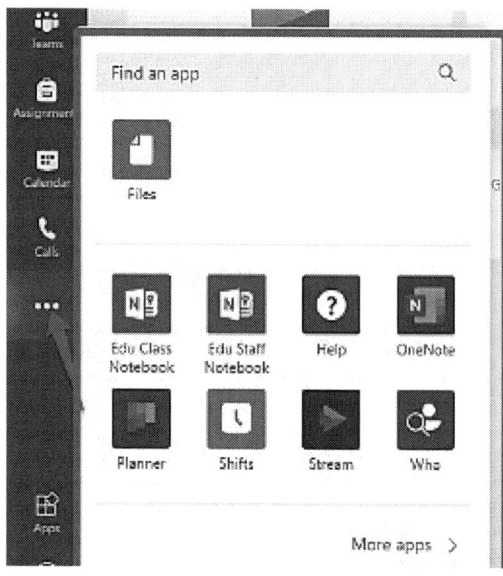

If you don't have the Teams app installed already on your computer, you can do a quick download and carry out installation by clicking on the download tab below the navigation bar.

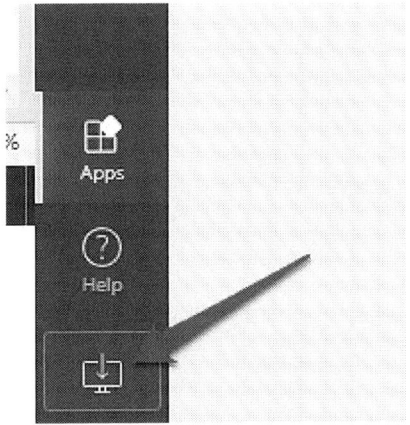

THE PROFILE BUTTON

At the top right corner of your screen is your profile button.

Usually, you can upload your picture there to display during a chat or video meetings.

There are a couple of features you can access by clicking on the profile picture. Which includes;

- **Setting your user status**

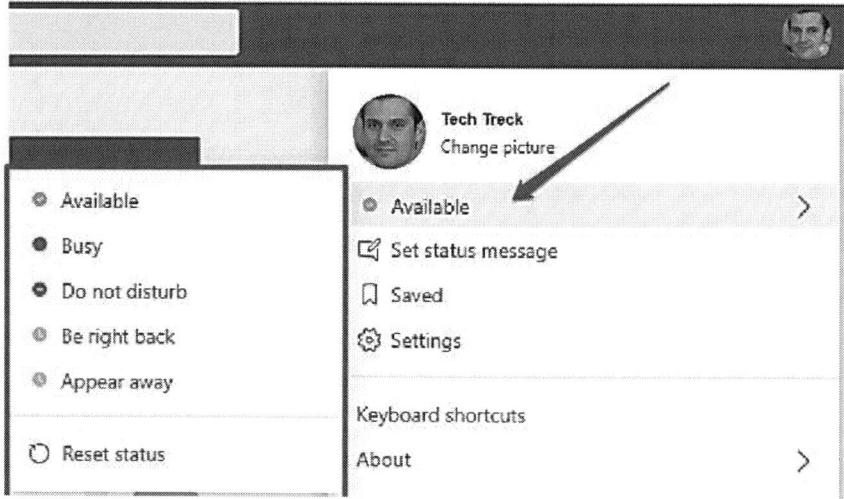

When having a chat with your students in Teams, your status allows them to know if you are busy or available.

- **Set status message**

Set status message allows you to create a customized auto-respond message when someone sends you a message.

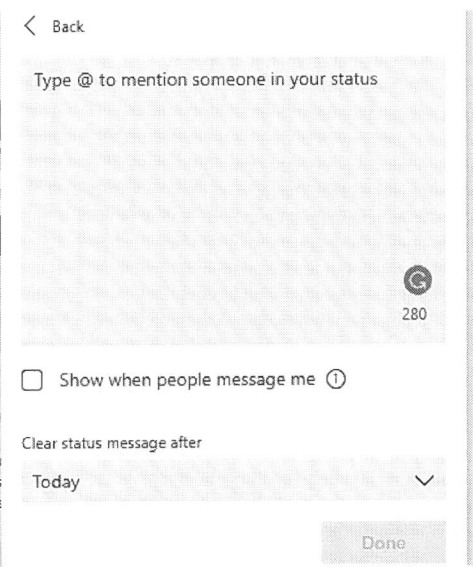

- ***Saved*** takes you to all your stored private conversations.

LESSON THREE

TEAMS AND CHANNELS FEATURES

Microsoft Teams for Education is built from scratch with the modern classroom in mind.

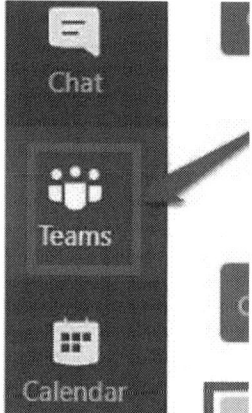

Think of **Teams** as your *Classroom*.

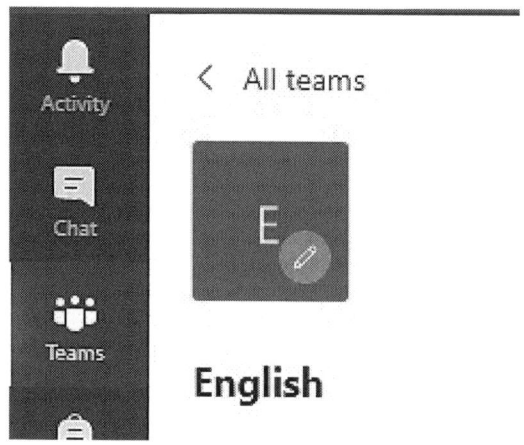

In Microsoft Teams for Education, you work in different "*teams/ classrooms*". You can think of each team as a class where you teach several subjects together with your students. Every student who is a member of the classroom will be included in everything that goes on in the class.

Teams also show as classrooms you have been invited to join.

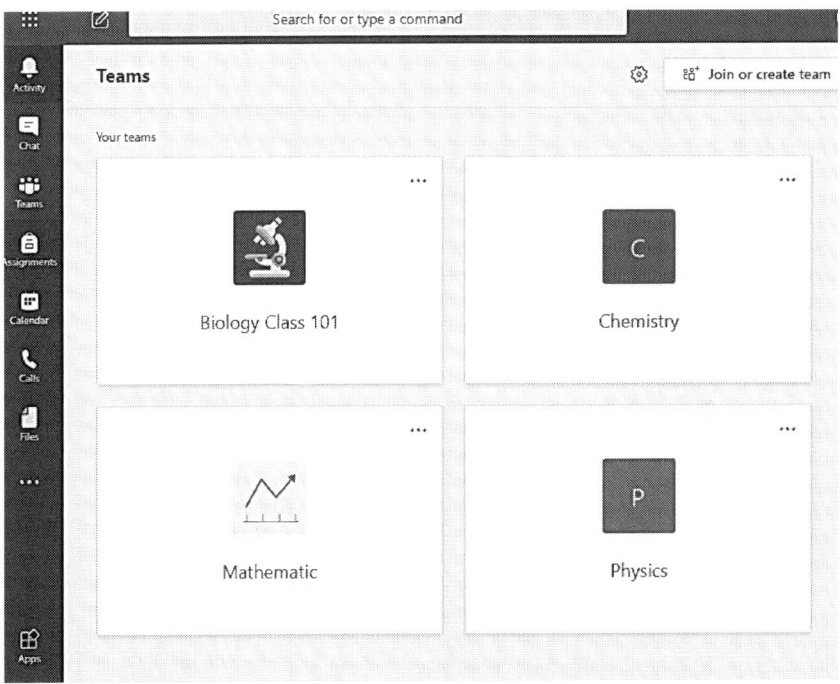

Each Team has a distinct name to differentiate one from the other on your screen. Even if you can "walk between different classrooms", it can be a bit confusing and exhausting. Similarly, in Microsoft Teams for Education, you don't want to create or join too many classrooms.

Before using Microsoft Teams for Education you should consider how various classes within your school collaborate. Plan how you want to create your classroom as a teacher for effective collaboration.

When a Team or classroom is created, only students added to the Teams or with invitation codes can join and have access to discussions, meetings, and resource documents.

CHANNELS IN TEAMS AND HOW THEY FUNCTION

When you first create a Teams or Class, it automatically creates a room referred to as *General* in Microsoft Teams for Education.

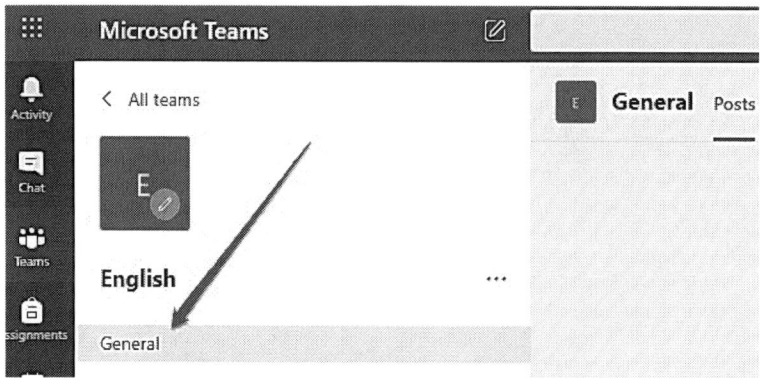

Think of this room as a *Channel*.

In this *General* room or channel, you can view every interaction made by your students even when you are not online. These interactions among your students in a channel can be *Posts*, *Conversations*, *Announcements*, and *Replies* within your Microsoft Teams for Education app. Every activity is visible within the "Posts" tab. Everyone in the team sees everything in the General channel Posts.

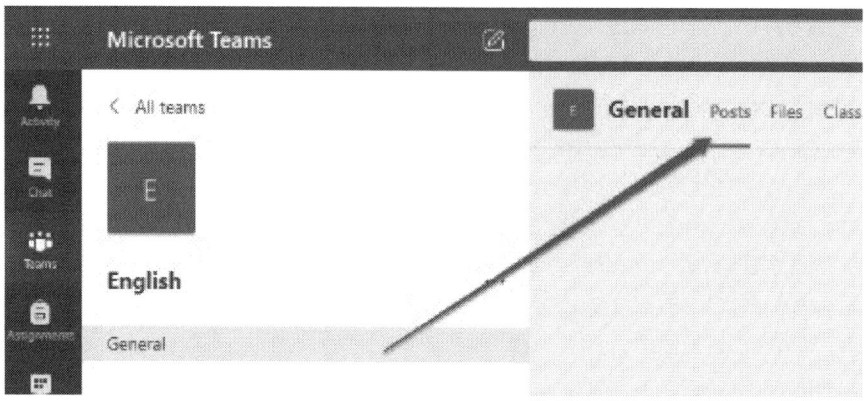

You are not limited to just sending messages to your students in the General Channel or room. You also have access to facial expressions and body language.

In Microsoft Teams for Education, members can express themselves using emoticons, GIFs, stickers, memes, and much more.

The ability for teachers and students to express themselves more at will in a digital classroom makes it easier for members of a Team to let their personalities shine through.

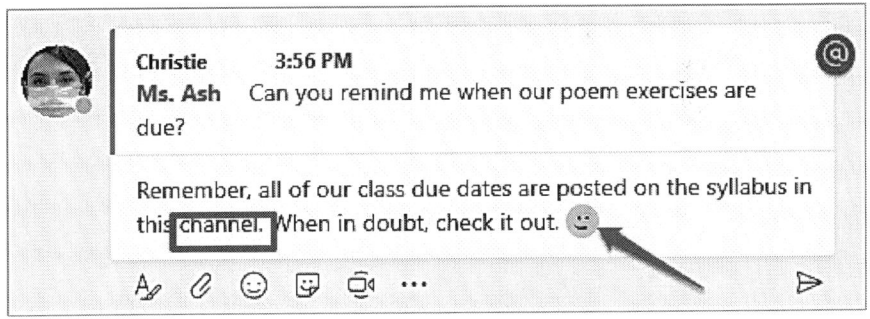

As you start teaching more classes or subjects and join more Teams, different constellations of students in your school will break out and start working on different Channels. This means you will need to create new channels to maintain an organized classroom.

23

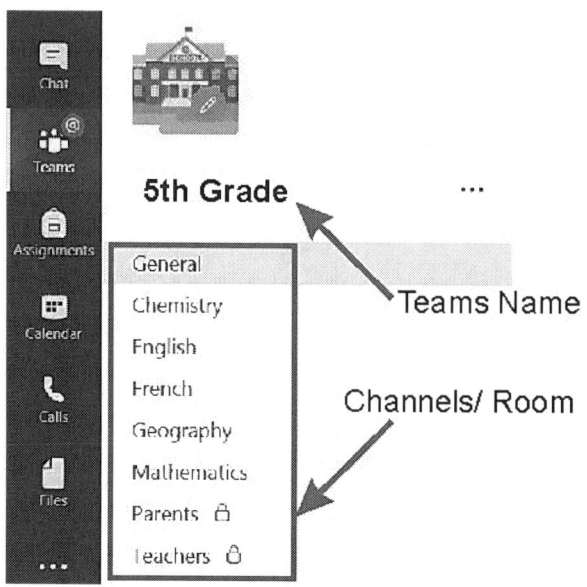

You can create a channel and decide if that channel should be "*Standard*" or "*Private*". A Private channel is not accessible to everyone in your team, only selected students in your teams/ class can see and have access.

ACTIVITY FEED FOR TEACHERS AND STUDENTS

The Activity tab is the first on the navigation bar and can be referred to as your hallway.

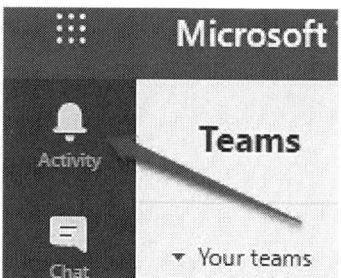

You can stand in the hallway, open the doors to the classroom or Teams, and view all the conversations going on in various Teams you belong to– without leaving the hallway.

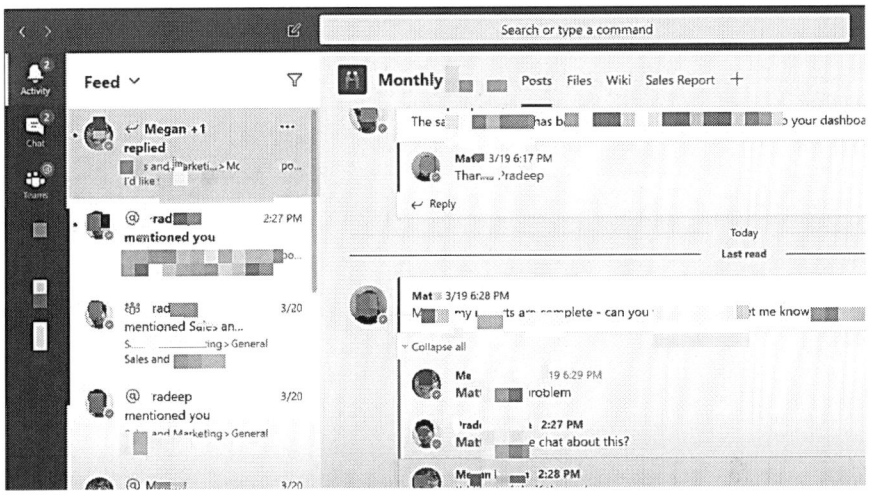

The Activity tab consolidates all the activity from your different teams, channels, and chats all in one place.

Whenever you are looking for a conversation or a topic you discussed and files shared with your students, you can have them all recorded and stored in the *Activity* feed.

As activities go on in your channels, you and your students will see a red number icon over the activity tab.

The number icon with a red circle and a number is a way to notify members of a team about activities happening that is yet to be seen or read. The feeds in the Activity tab show all that is going on in your channels. Once you click on the tab, the *number icon* notifications will be removed.

25

@MENTIONS

You or your students and other members of a Team can attract someone's attention by using the **@mention** feature.

Whenever someone @mentions a member of a Teams, they will see it in their "Activity feed" whether they have turned on channel notifications or not.

CHATS

Chat within Teams is like using Skype or any chat apps. Teachers can exchange text chats, video, and audio calls with one or more students or co-teacher. Chats can be private or open conversations between teachers and students who are members of a team.

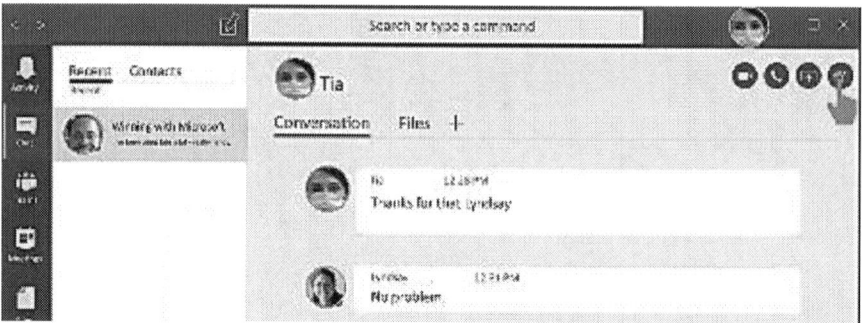

Sometimes you may have the need to have a private conversation with some of your students, or a group and not heard by everyone else. As a teacher, use "Chat" or "Calls" for private conversation by creating group chats.

Meanwhile, it is advisable not to use private chats for discussions that could be of interest to other students in the channel. Such discussions should be made in the channel posts, where they can be seen by others.

TABS

Tabs in Microsoft Teams are like posters pinned on a wall. Teachers can use tabs in all channels they create to post information, documents, or apps, to help members of your channel focus on.

LESSON FOUR

PERMISSION AND SECURITY IN TEAMS

Keeping track of how your students or members can access information and member's capabilities within Microsoft Teams is a great place to start. Microsoft Teams' permission is based on member's and owner's status of the Teams and Group.

Owners such as a teacher have access to the Teams settings. Owners can add or remove students from a Team. The administrative privilege is also given to the owner of a team.

By default, students who are part of a Team cannot access or change Team settings or add members. As a teacher who is the owner of a Teams, you can edit the application and create lists and libraries. Students can also create channels in Teams if permitted.

Both Teachers and students (by default) can connect external applications such as storage and collaboration apps–to each Team via Team channel tabs. Teachers and students can also add tabs to Teams channels and delete them.

With external sharing activated from the admin center, teachers can invite "Guest" users like parents or external supervisors from outside the school to Teams. Guest users in Teams can participate in private chats but by default can not add or remove channels or tabs. Guest users also don't have access to Teams conversations for joined Teams.

RESTRICTIONS ON PRIVATE OR PUBLIC CHANNELS

WHAT ARE PRIVATE CHANNELS?

Only a private channel owner and members can access private channel conversation, other team members don't have access to the conversation and files.

As a teacher, if you are not a member of a private channel, you won't have access to the private channel site collection and conversation.

Private channels owners like teachers or administrators can approve membership or add students directly. Information stored in private Teams might or may not be accessible by the school admin depending on Teams Settings. The information within a private Team does not appear in search results by default. Nevertheless, the Team name, description, and the student and teacher who owns the Team can be seen by users.

BREAKOUT GROUPS OR PRIVATE CHANNEL

Click on the 3-dots beside the Team's name and click on *Add Channel.*

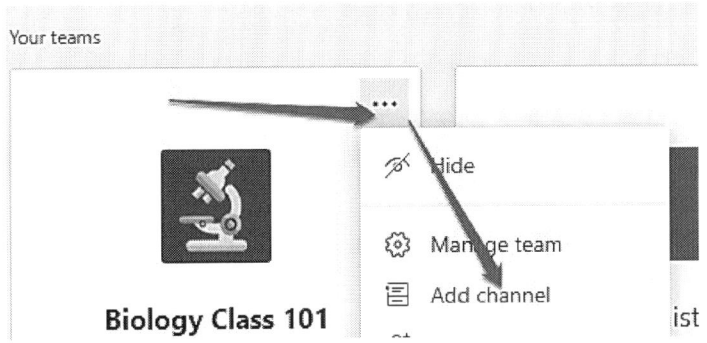

Next, Enter the Name of the channel and description.

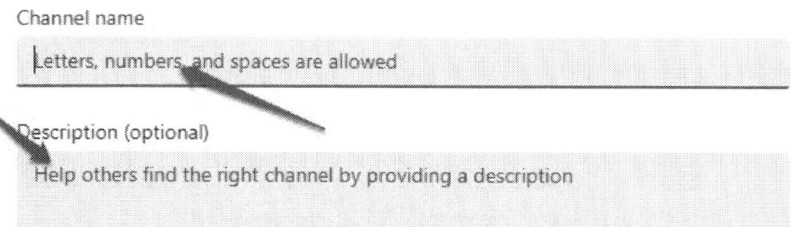

When you get to the Privacy section, change it to Private.

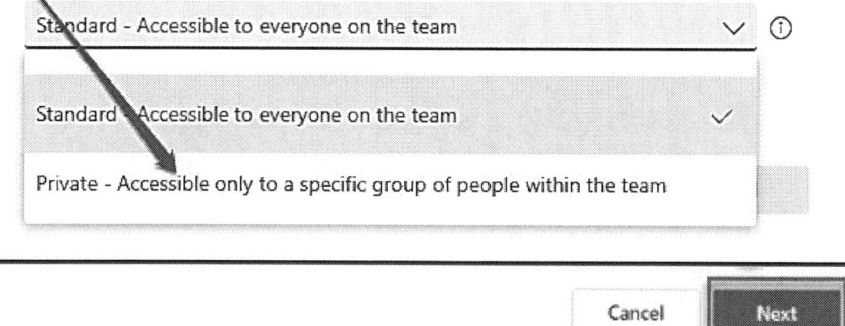

Click on the Next button to add students or skip to create the channel.

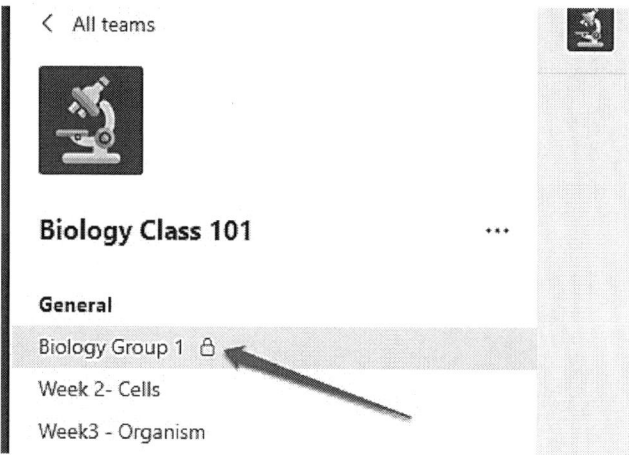

A private Channel has a padlock icon beside its name.

HOW TO MANAGE PRIVATE CHANNELS.

Each private channel in your teams has unique members and settings. As a teacher who owns the Team, you can manage students and the channel settings from the Manage channel option. This you do by clicking on the 3-dots beside the private channel.

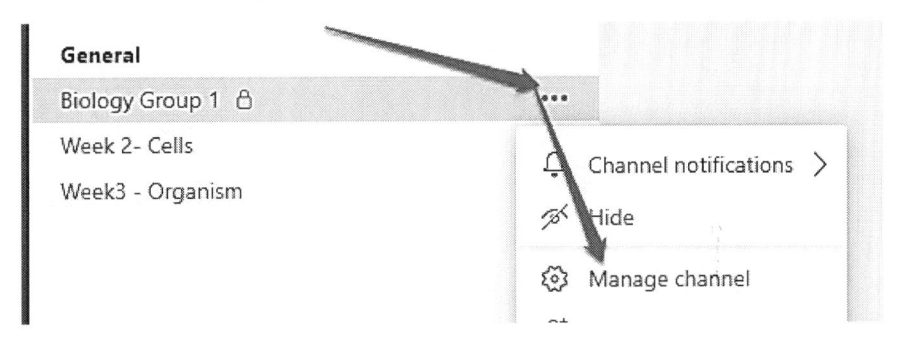

ADDING MEMBERS TO A PRIVATE CHANNEL

Teachers can add or remove students from a private channel. When you click on the Manage channel option, the next tab displays a list of students already added to your private channel. Teachers can add members only from the existing Team members list.

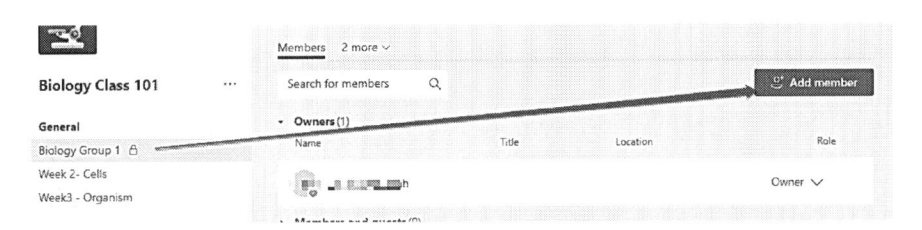

If a team owner removes any student or member from the parent team, such a student or member will automatically be removed from all private channels in the team.

PRIVATE CHANNEL SETTINGS

Each private channel has its settings, which includes:

- Member Permission (settings for tabs and message)
- @mentions
- Fun Stuff (settings for Giphy, Stickers, Memes)

To access the settings tab, click on Manage channel, and click on Settings.

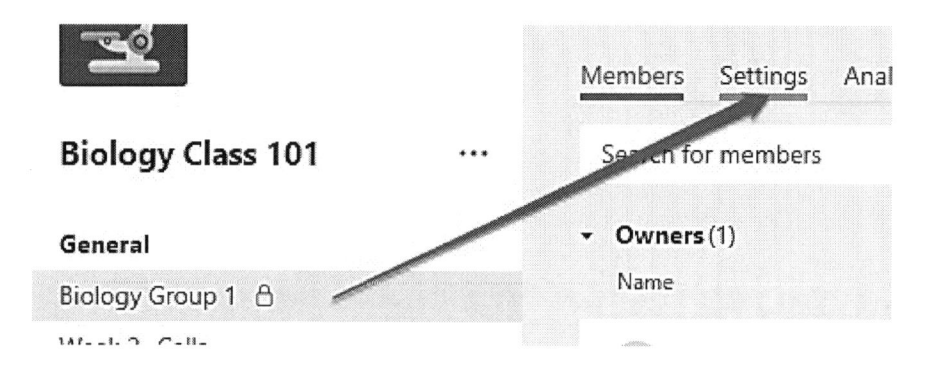

This will display the settings tab.

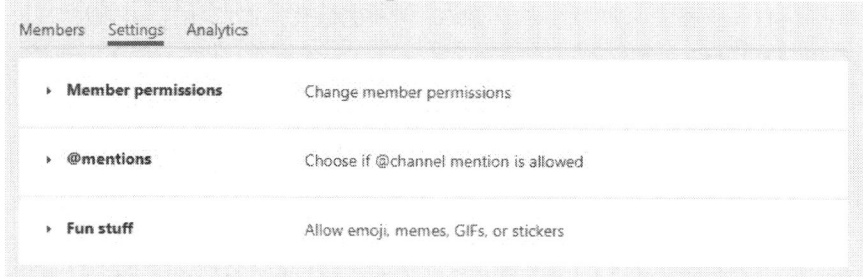

The above setting does not depend on parent team settings. For example, the @mention setting is enabled in parent team settings but in the private channel setting, it is disabled. So a student who is a member of the private channel can't use @mention in the particular channel, but the same student can use @mention in the other normal channels.

Each option under the Private channel settings has a drop-down feature that drops down when you click on the black arrow.

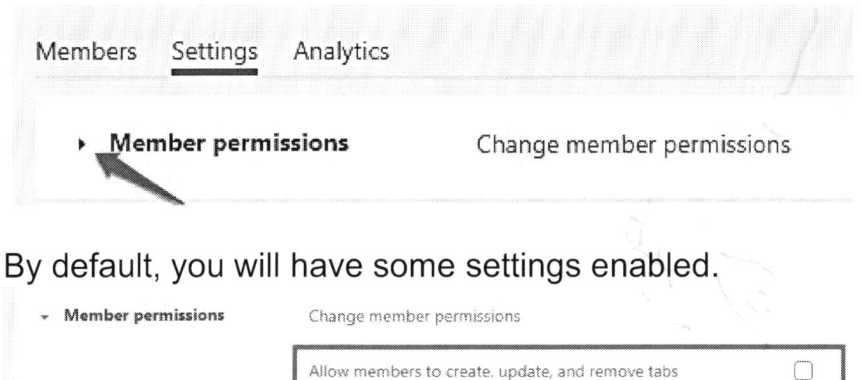

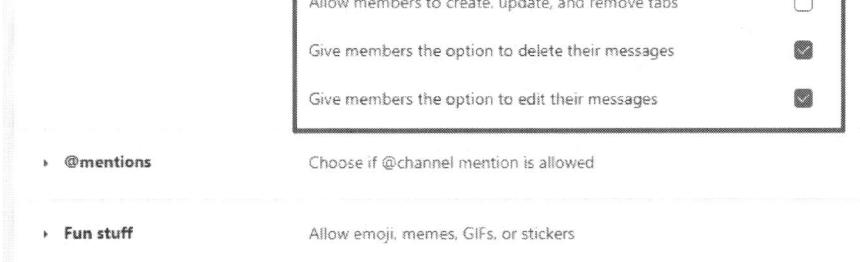

By default, you will have some settings enabled.

You can disable or enable the settings you want.

PRIVATE CHANNEL PEOPLE PANE

People pane options will display all students who are members of your private channel.

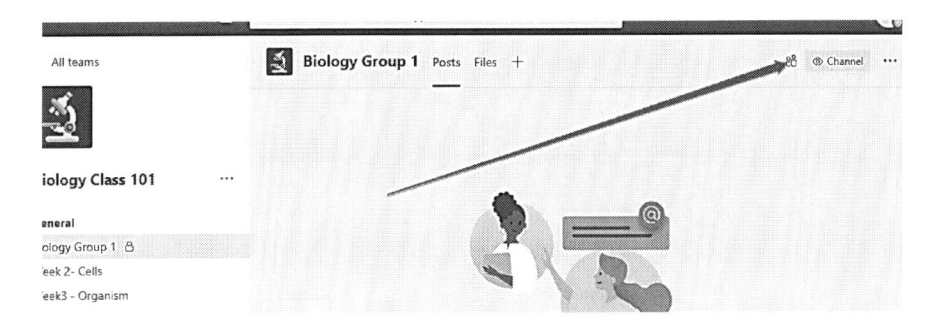

Only private channel owners and members can see the people panel. A private channel admin can add the user from the people's pane option by click on the Add member button located at the bottom left corner of the screen.

PRIVATE CHANNEL FILE MANAGEMENT

Each private channel has its site collection with its name displayed like *"Parent Team Name"- "Private Channel Name"*.

For example, If the parent team name is Biology Group 101 and private channel name is Group1, then the corresponding site collection name will be displayed as *Biology Group 101 – Group 1*

Every private channel file is linked with the corresponding site collection document library. If you delete the private channel, the corresponding site collection will also be removed from SharePoint online and moved to the recycle bin.

If you later restore the private channel, the corresponding site collection will also be restored. Members can not be added directly to a Private channel site collection.

STUDENTS, AND GUESTS AND EXTERNAL GUEST

Guest access allows teachers to add parents of their students to teams and channels in Microsoft Teams. Although, any guest with a business or consumer email accounts, such as Gmail or Yahoo, can participate as a Teams guest with full access to team meetings, chats, and resource documents. However, they won't be able to create meetings, add apps, or share chat files. Teams admin can assign features that guests can use in Teams, such as stickers or memes in conversation, and so on.

External access is granted to someone that does not have a relationship with your school that uses Teams to be able to find and contact you through your email address.

TEAMS MEMBER PERMISSION

As a teacher and owner of a team, you can manage member's permission settings from individual teams.

Click on any of your Teams, click on the 3-dots, and select Manage teams.

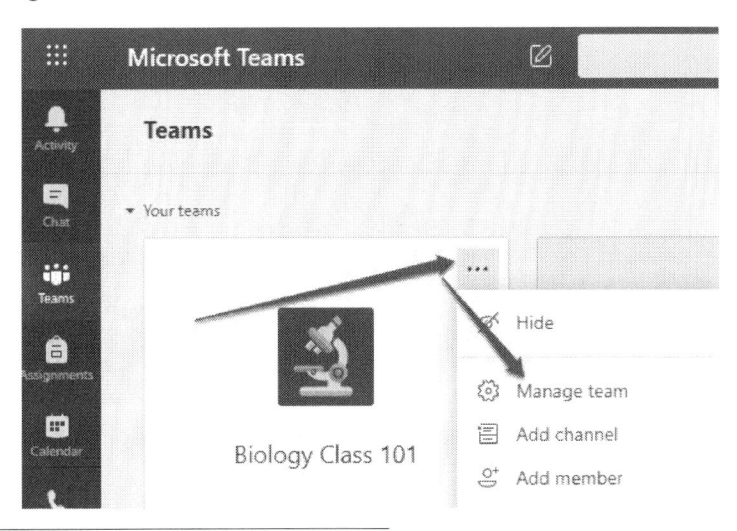

Each team setting is independent of the other.

Next, click on Settings.

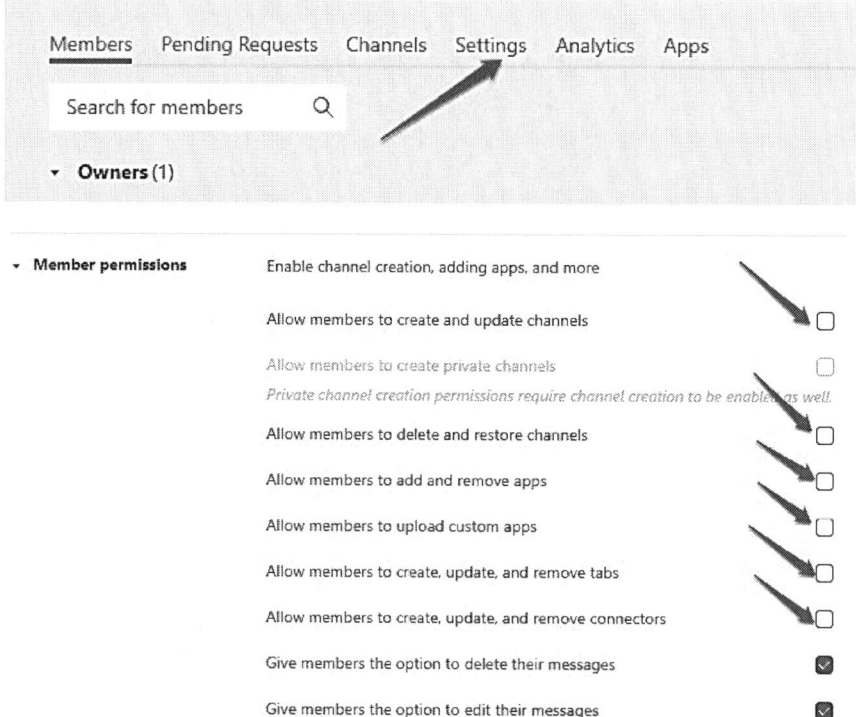

| Members | Pending Requests | Channels | Settings | Analytics | Apps |

Search for members

▼ **Owners** (1)

▼ **Member permissions** Enable channel creation, adding apps, and more

Allow members to create and update channels ☐

Allow members to create private channels ☐
Private channel creation permissions require channel creation to be enabled as well.

Allow members to delete and restore channels ☐

Allow members to add and remove apps ☐

Allow members to upload custom apps ☐

Allow members to create, update, and remove tabs ☐

Allow members to create, update, and remove connectors ☐

Give members the option to delete their messages ☑

Give members the option to edit their messages ☑

To have total control over your teams and channel as a teacher, the following settings should be disabled as indicated above.
- Students to Create Channels and Add Apps
- Students to Create and Update Channels
- Student to Delete and Restore Channels
- Students to Add and Remove Apps
- Students to Create, Update and Remove Tabs
- Student to Create, Update and Remove Connectors

LESSON FIVE

CLASSROOMS AS TEAMS

It is important to have your classroom properly set up and organize from the beginning. As earlier discussed, your Teams is like a classroom, while your channels and tab allow you to work in separate groups. In every Team, you work with Channels, Tabs, and Apps. Your ability to make use of each of these components of your Teams is vital to use Microsoft Teams for Education effectively.

There are four types of Teams in Microsoft Teams for Education, which includes: Classes, PLCs, Staff Members, and Others.

Microsoft Teams allows teachers to create multiple teams. Meanwhile, it is important to know the differences between each type of Team.

CLASS TEAMS

Class Teams are created to add students and co-teachers as members. Each class team is independent and allows instructors to create quizzes, assignments, record collect student feedback. There is also provision for teachers to give students who are members of a team private space for notes in Class Notebook. If you are an elementary teacher, you will have one team for each section within team. Teams can be created for each class or subject you teach. Only students added to each of your teams can have access to features and resources assigned to such teams they are part of.

TEAM FOR EDUCATORS WORKGROUP/ PROFESSIONAL LEARNING COMMUNITY

Educators work together on shared goals or professional development. PLC team allows you to organize materials, collaborate, and access a OneNote notebook populated with templates for common PLC tasks. Use this team if you are collaborating with other team members as a Professional Learning Community.

TEAM FOR STAFF/ SCHOOL ADMINISTRATION AND DEVELOPMENT

Staff leaders own staff teams and add others as members, which allows you to communicate, share important documents, and set up a Staff Notebook to track common administrative goals. Use this team if you are collaborating with other team members or administration on projects.

Any Group Team
Educators or students can create teams to work together on any shared goal, project, or activity. Use this team if you are collaborating with other teams members or administration on projects.

HOW TO CREATE A CLASS TEAM

As a teacher, once you can log into Microsoft Teams on either your device or web platform, you can begin to create your first Class by clicking on the **Team tab** and then click on **Create team** button.

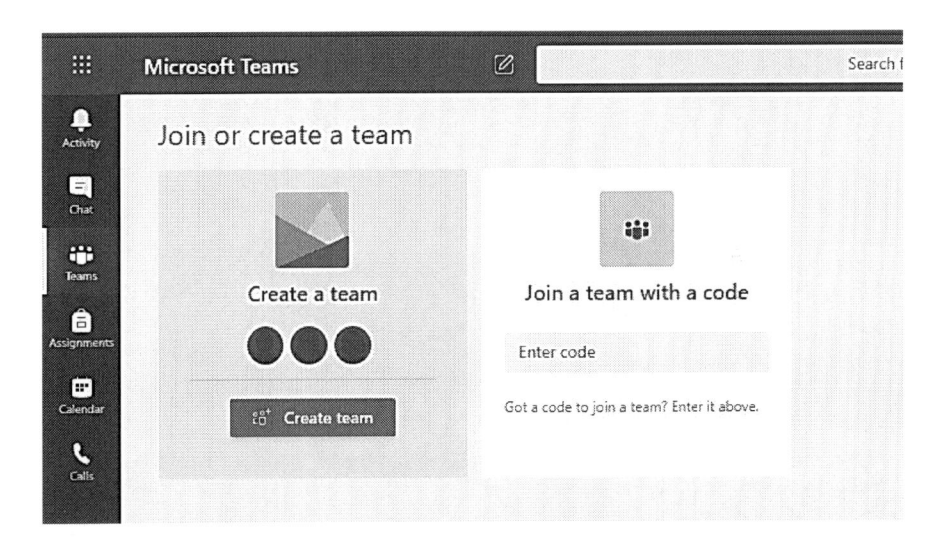

From the Teams template, click on **Class,** then click on **Create** to continue.

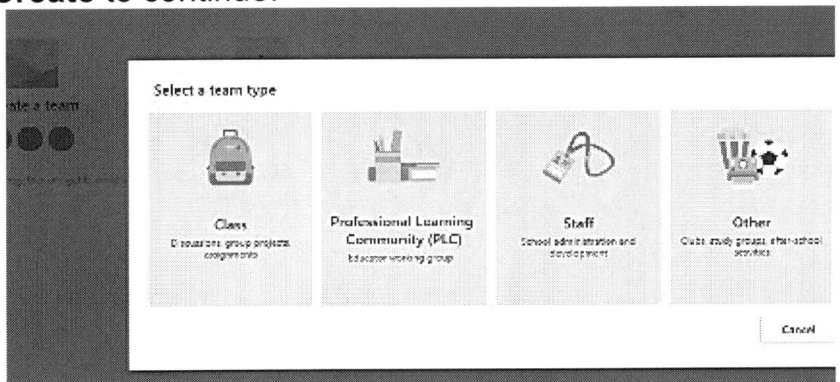

Next, you enter the name of your Team and its description.

Create your team

Teachers are owners of class teams and students participate as members. Each class team allows you to create assignments and quizzes, record student feedback, and give your students a private space for notes in Class Notebook.

Name

Description (optional)

Cancel   Next

Although, adding a description of your teams is optional, if added will help your students understand which of the teams they are going into.

Create your team

Teachers are owners of class teams and students participate as members. Each class team allows you to create assignments and quizzes, record student feedback, and give your students a private space for notes in Class Notebook.

Name

Biology 101

Description (optional)

We will continue the class from last week........

Cancel   **Next**

Click on **Next** to continue.

The next screen allows you to add students or co-teachers to your teams. To add people to your teams, you type their name or email address and it will appear as a list for you to choose from. This list is gotten from those whose details are stored in your school contact database under Office 365.

Add people to "Test 1"

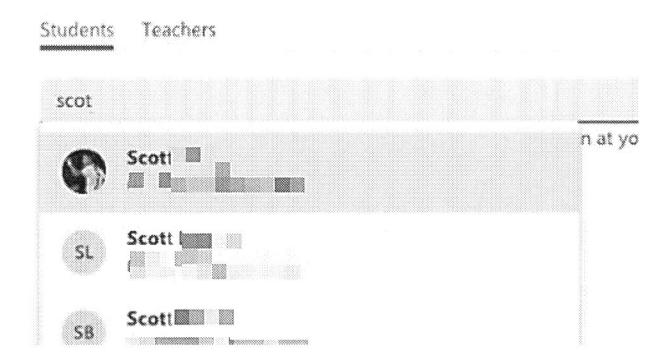

Students Teachers

scot

Scott

Scott

Scott

If you have a large class, you may need to click on the *Skip* **button**.

Skip

The new Teams or classroom will now appear on the second frame beside the Navigation panel.

Microsoft Teams

All teams

B1

Biology 101

General

By default, your new team is **Private**, so only those you add to the teams can have access to its contents. On the second frame are tools you can use to boost your Team productivity.

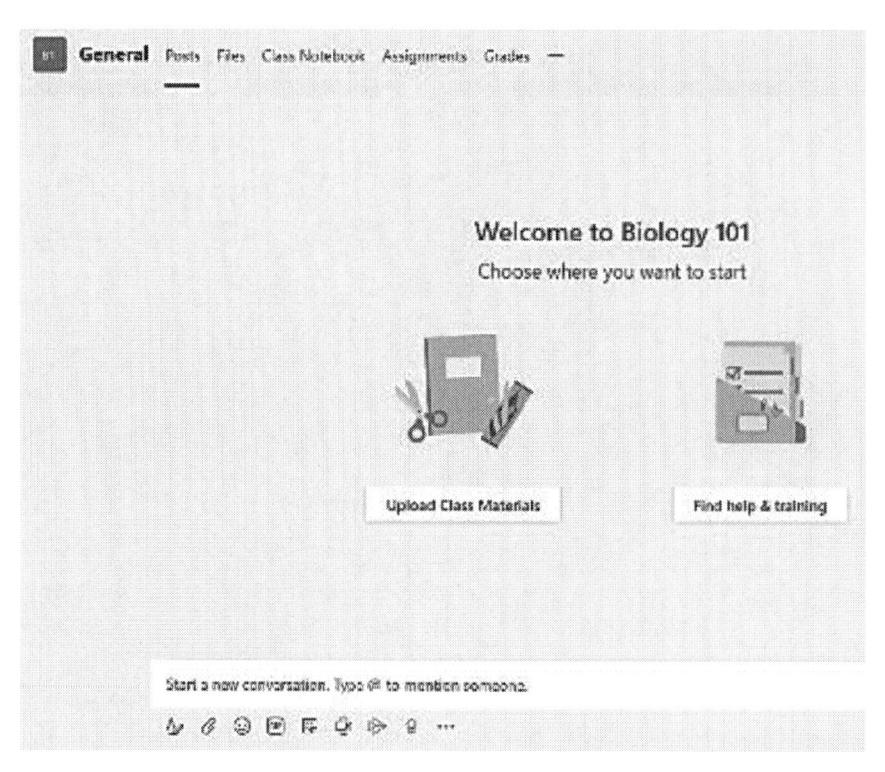

By default, a **Channel** called *General* is automatically created.

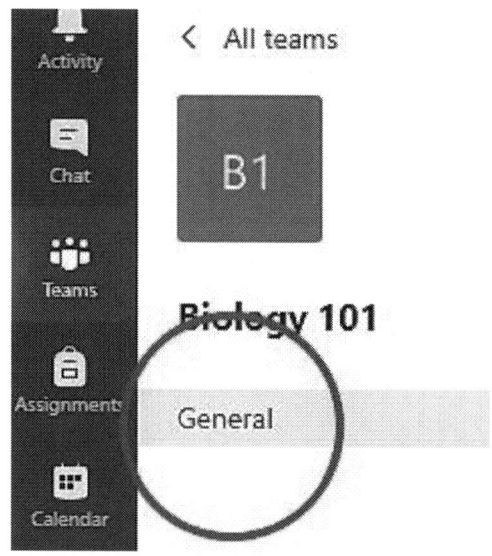

42

When in a class Team, you are taken to the *General* channel which is where your students or co-teachers can ask questions, share resources, and have class discussions.

The General channel is like a social media platform, where members of your teams can reply and leave emoji.

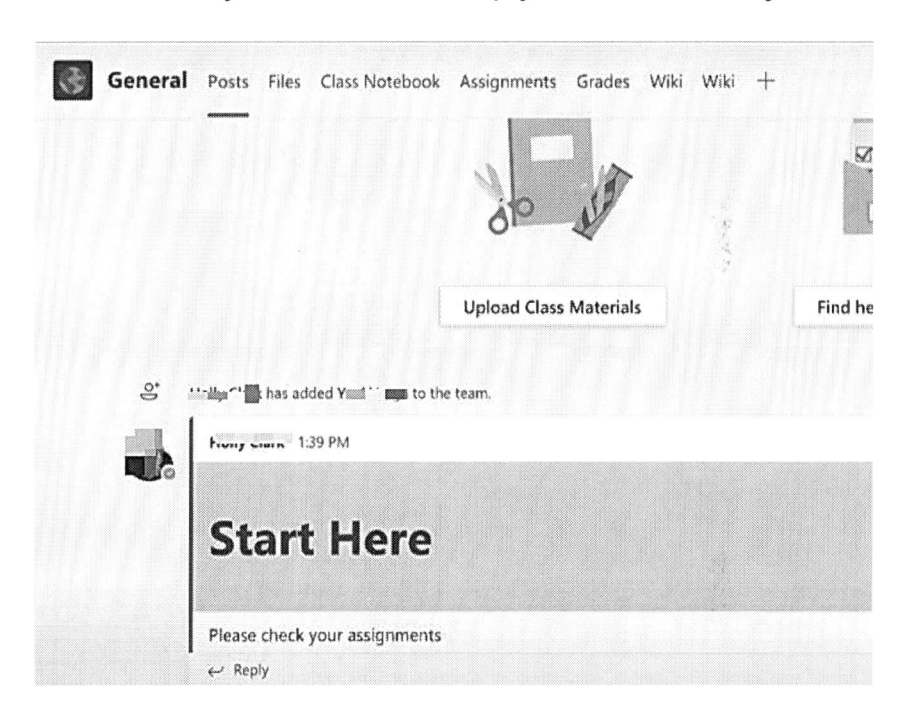

HOW TO CHANGE DISPLAY ICON OF A CLASS TEAM

If you wish to change the display picture of your Team, click on the three dots beside the icon and select *Edit team.*

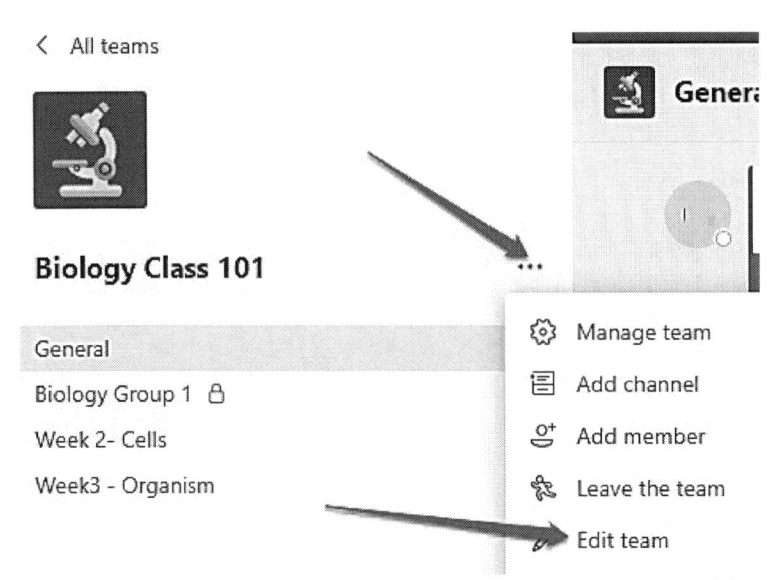

Select the icon you wish to use and click on the Update button to complete the process.

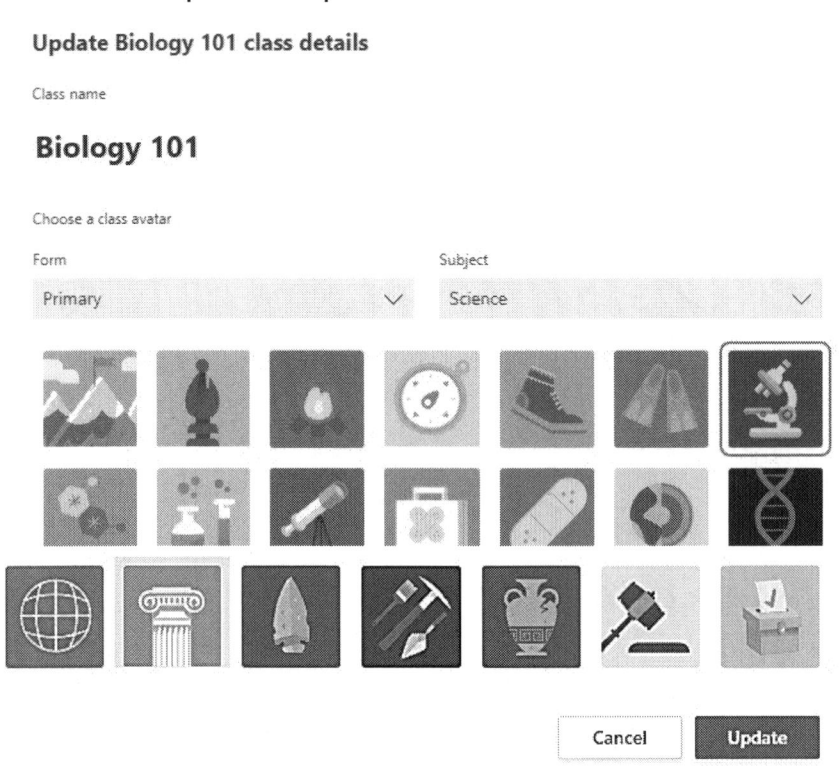

HOW TO CHANGE YOUR CLASS NAME

To change the name you gave to your Class Team, use the three dots beside the Teams name, then select Edit teams. Next, edit the name of your team and click on the update button to complete the process.

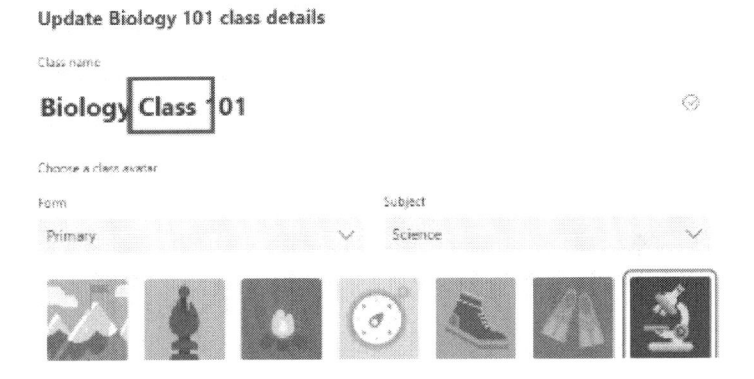

Changes made will appear immediately you click on the update button.

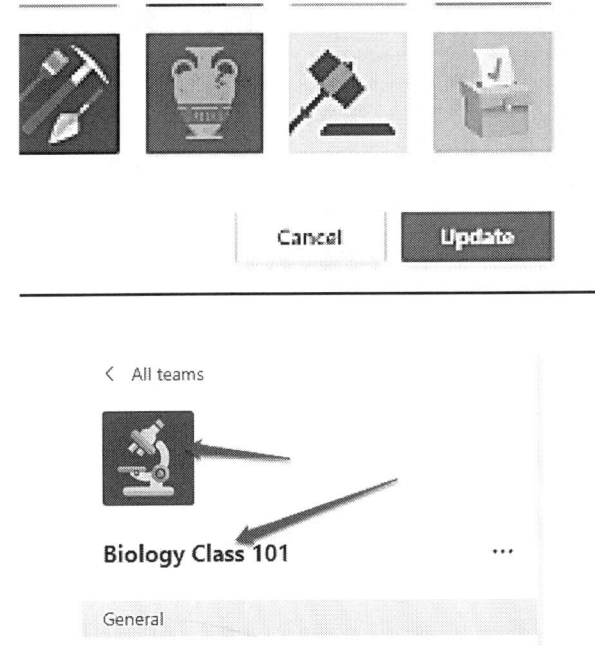

ADDING STUDENTS TO YOUR CLASS TEAM

To add students to your class team, click on the three-dots beside the Teams icon, and select **Add members.**

Next, go on and start searching your students one after the other.

Another way to add members to your teams is through the Teams management interface. This time, after clicking on the three-dots, select **Manage Team.** There you will be able to see a list of students who are members of your team.

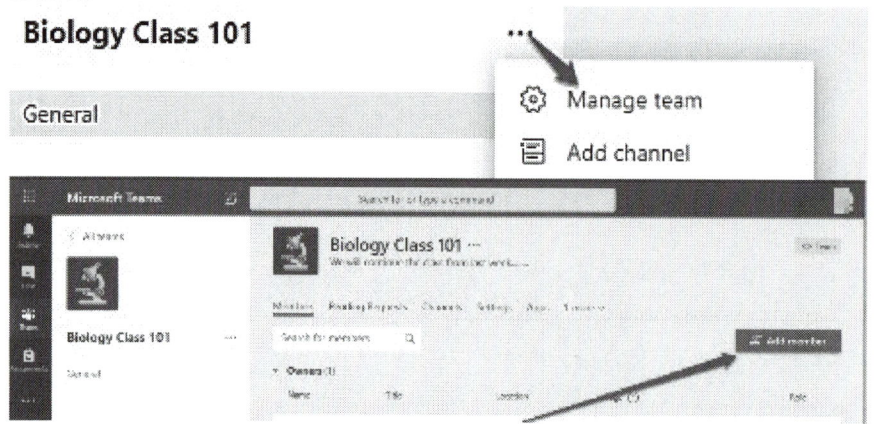

To add more members, click on the **Add member** button.

USING CODE TO ADD STUDENTS TO A CLASS TEAMS

Class teams should be ready before giving your students or co-teachers the codes to join the Teams.

To create a Team code, click on the 3-dots, and select Manage Teams.

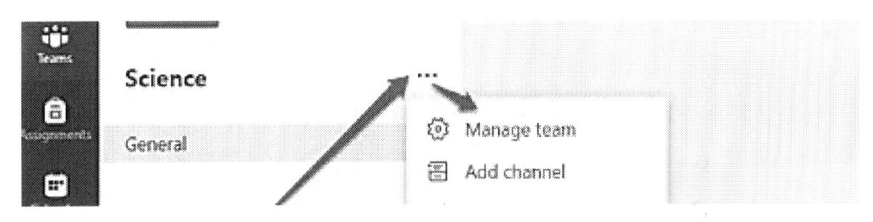

Click on the Settings tab,

Click on Team code, then click on the Generate button.

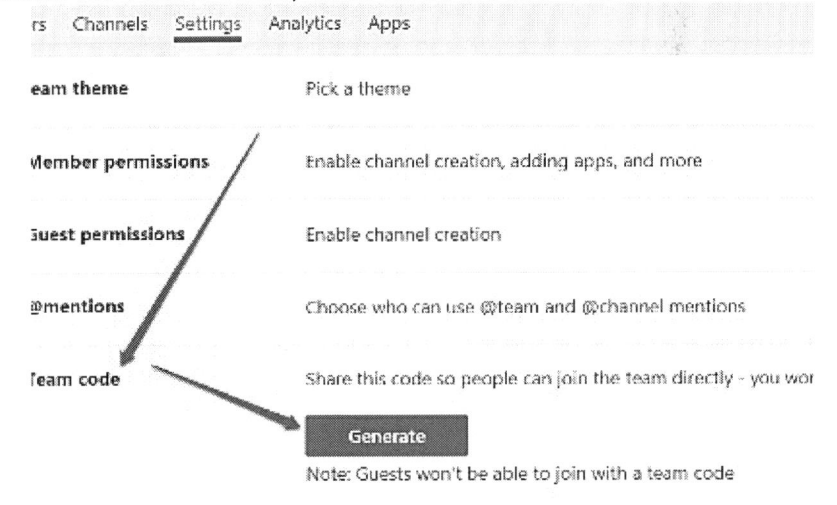

You will be given a code for the class. Copy and send the code in a mail to your students to join your Microsoft Teams.

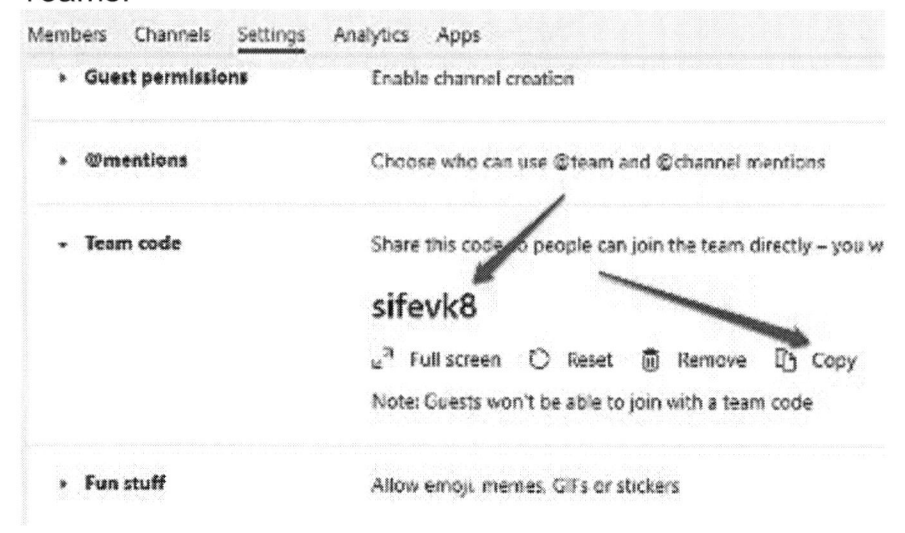

Members	Channels	Settings	Analytics	Apps
▸ **Guest permissions**		Enable channel creation		
▸ **@mentions**		Choose who can use @team and @channel mentions		
▾ **Team code**		Share this code so people can join the team directly – you w **sifevk8** Full screen Reset Remove Copy Note: Guests won't be able to join with a team code		
▸ **Fun stuff**		Allow emoji, memes, GIFs or stickers		

To share the code with your students, you can simply send a mail to them. Copy and paste the join code and team link into the mail.

CREATING A CLASS CHANNEL IN TEAMS

As a best practice, to create a channel for each week or topic that you have as an essential part of the lesson and course that you will be teaching. To add a new channel to the already existing General channel, click on the three-dots and select **Add Channel.**

Biology Class 101

Give you channel a name and choose if you like to make is Private or accessible to everyone on the team.

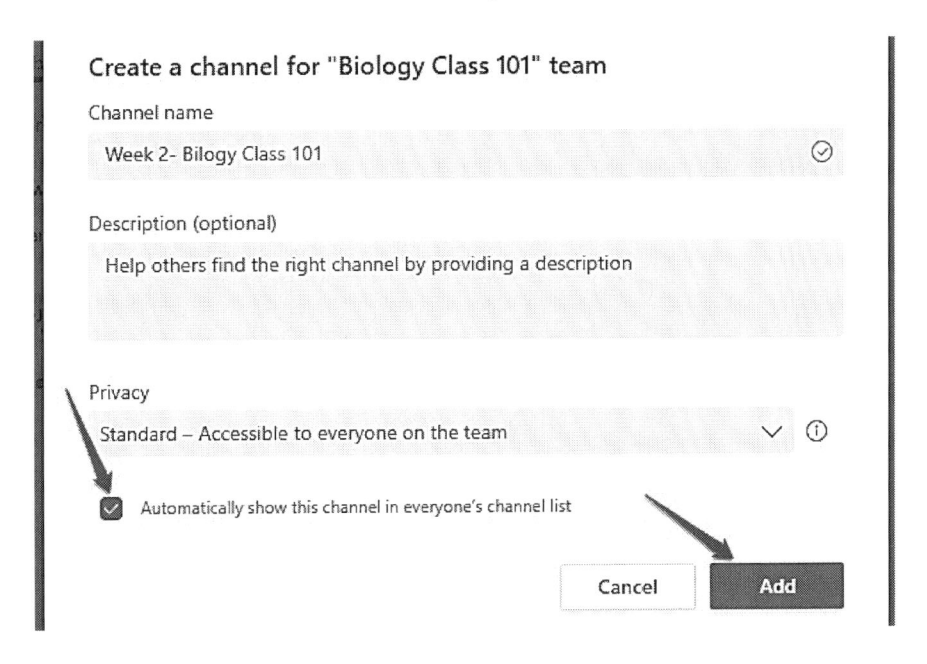

Create a channel for "Biology Class 101" team

Channel name

Week 2- Bilogy Class 101

Description (optional)

Help others find the right channel by providing a description

Privacy

Standard – Accessible to everyone on the team

☑ Automatically show this channel in everyone's channel list

Cancel   Add

If your channel is **Standard,** click on the Automatically show this channel in everyone's channel list to have it pinned so your students see it on the left-hand side of the app.

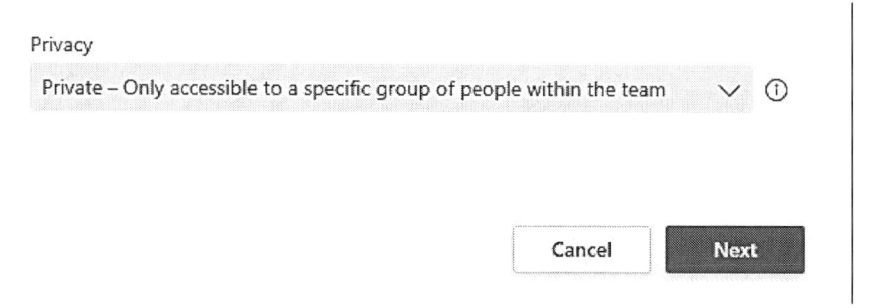

If you choose to make your channel private, you will need to add students to it manually.

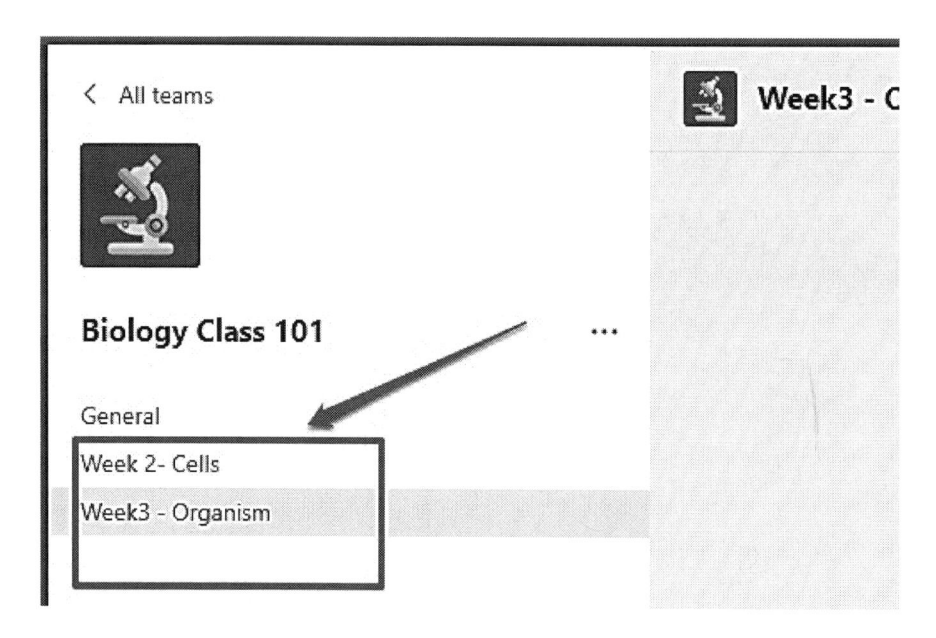

Every channel created has an independent collaboration space to post a message to students who have access. Classwork can be discussed, allowing both teachers and students to add their input to the discussion like a social media platform. Along the line, files can be shared as for reference purposes, students can also reply to messages using emojis to express their feelings.

By default, a newly created channels come with three tabs automatically created; Posts, Files, and Notes tab.

Week 2- Cells   Posts   Files   Notes   +

Tabs enable you to upload, review, edit files, notes, and customized content (such as word or pdf documents, spreadsheets, presentations, videos, external links, other applications, and more). This content is then easily accessible to everyone in the class.

The **post tab** is like a wall on a social media platform. Multiple conversations can be carried out with your students.

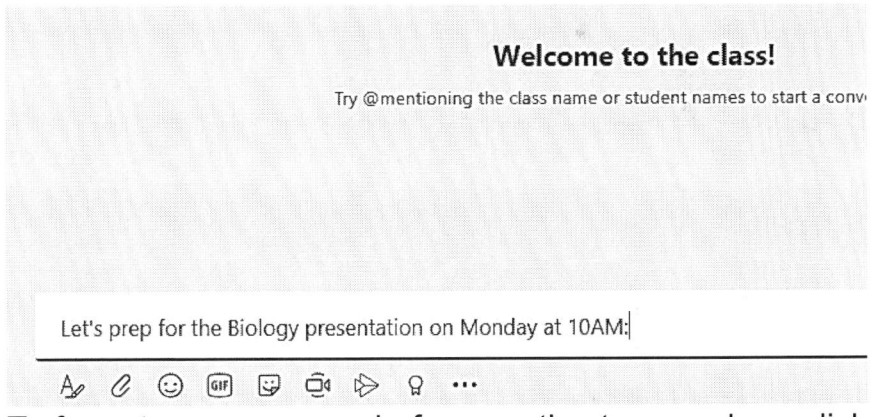

Welcome to the class!

Try @mentioning the class name or student names to start a conv

Let's prep for the Biology presentation on Monday at 10AM:

To format your message before posting to your class, click on the Format icon.

Let's prep for the Biol

This will pop up another interface for you to make your post more appealing to your students.

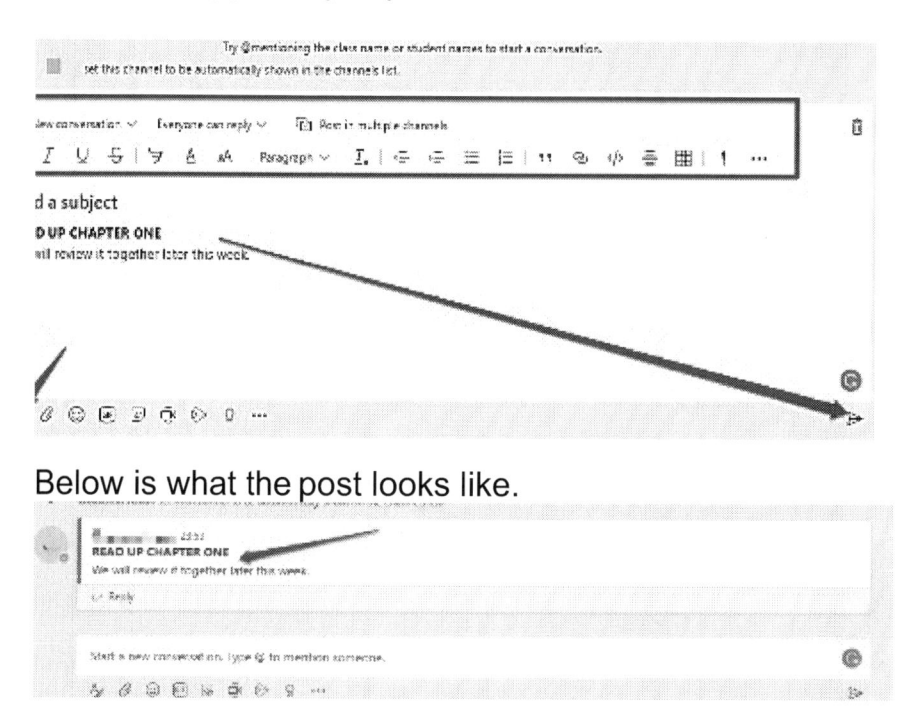

Below is what the post looks like.

ADDING TABS IN CHANNELS

As a teacher and owner of a team, only you can add or remove channel tabs by default within a Team. A teacher can modify this setting to permit all team members to add tabs if preferred. Creating a new tab requires clicking on the + button on the tab row.

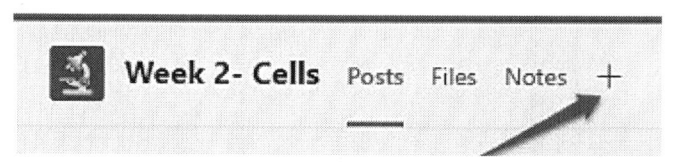

Next, you choose the app, services, or web page to add as a tab (some services require a paid subscription/license).

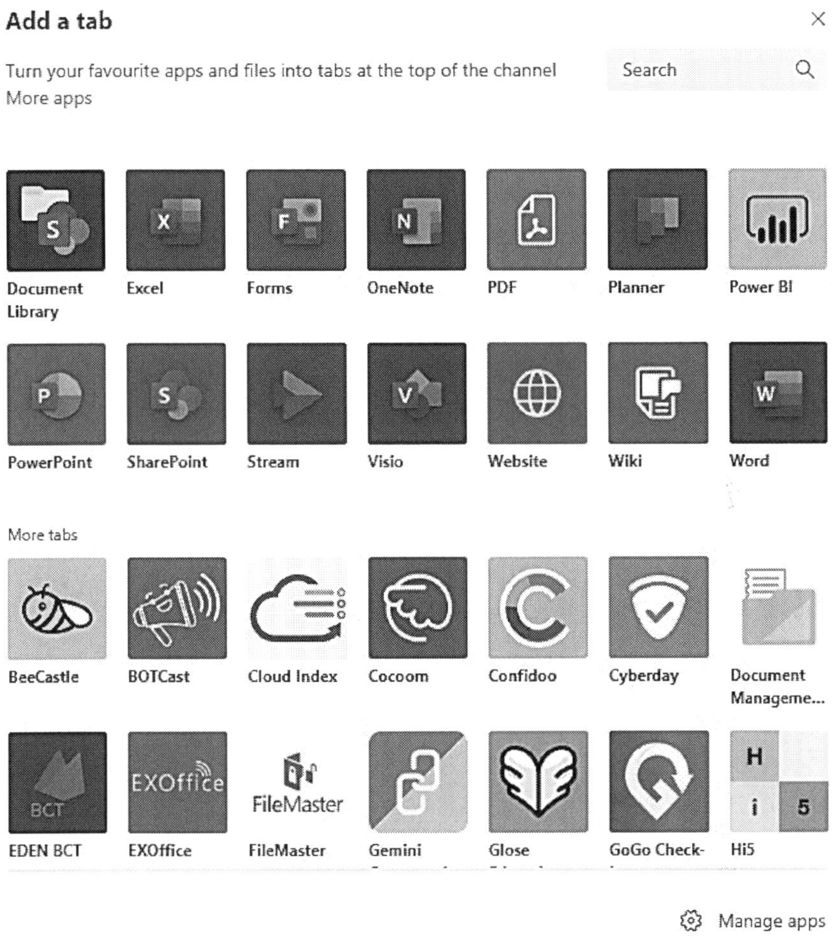

Add a tab

Turn your favourite apps and files into tabs at the top of the channel Search
More apps

| Document Library | Excel | Forms | OneNote | PDF | Planner | Power BI |

| PowerPoint | SharePoint | Stream | Visio | Website | Wiki | Word |

More tabs

| BeeCastle | BOTCast | Cloud Index | Cocoom | Confidoo | Cyberday | Document Manageme... |

| EDEN BCT | EXOffice | FileMaster | Gemini | Glose | GoGo Check- | Hi5 |

⚙ Manage apps

53

LESSON SIX

DOCUMENT MANAGEMENT

UPLOADING FILES TO STUDENTS

The files tab in any of your channels allows you to share files with your students. Such a file may be for reference purposes.

To any document in a channel, click on the Files tab.

Next, click on **Upload** and **browse** for the file you want to upload.

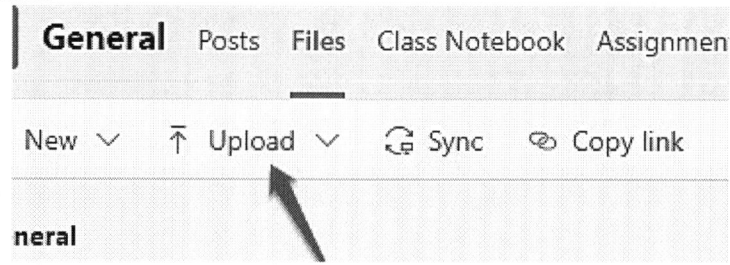

Another way to add a file is by using the drag and drop method. Once the file is completely uploaded, you will see it as a list. The more you upload your files, the more the list increases. Sometimes, you may like to share a link to the file you just uploaded to someone who is not a member of the Teams. Usee the *Copy link* button to get the link address and share it with anyone you want to have access to the file.

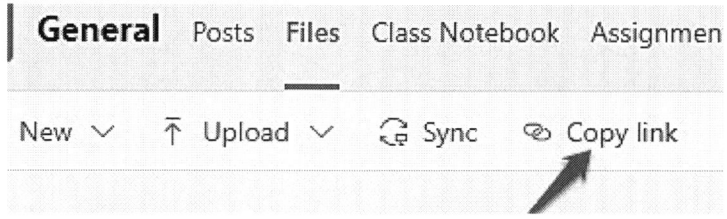

CREATING OFFICE 365 FILES FORMAT IN TEAMS

New files can be created without the need to upload into Microsoft Teams. Such files can be shared with students who are members of a team.

Under the Files tab in any of your channel, click on the arrow button beside *New* and select the file type from the dropdown list you want to create. By default, you can choose from; Word document, Excel spreadsheet, Powerpoint Presentation, OneNote, and Forms for Excel.

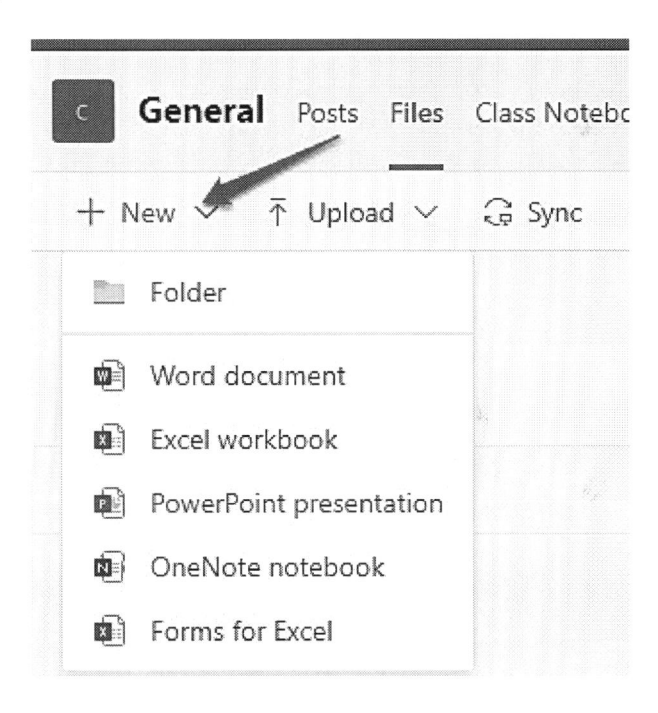

You can also create a folder to store your files in an organized way.

TRANSFER OR COPY FILES AND FOLDERS

Files or folders can be moved or copied to another location within your Microsoft Teams. To do this, locate the file you want to copy or move, highlight it, and then click on the 3-dots to choose the option you wish to use.

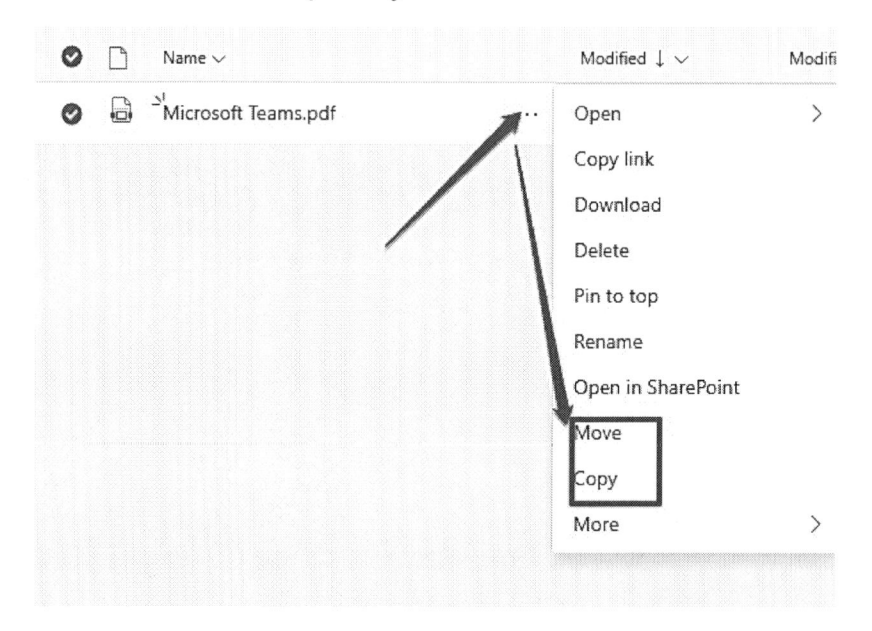

Click on the file or folder in the Files tab you want to move, then click on the 3-dots to choose the Move or Copy option.

COLLABORATING WITH A DOCUMENT IN TEAMS

Microsoft Teams can also be used to collaborate and engage in conversation about a resource document. As a teacher, you can upload a document and start a conversation with its content.

Alternatively, you can collaborate with your students using a document in the File tab of a specific channel.

Click on the File tab and click on the file to get started.

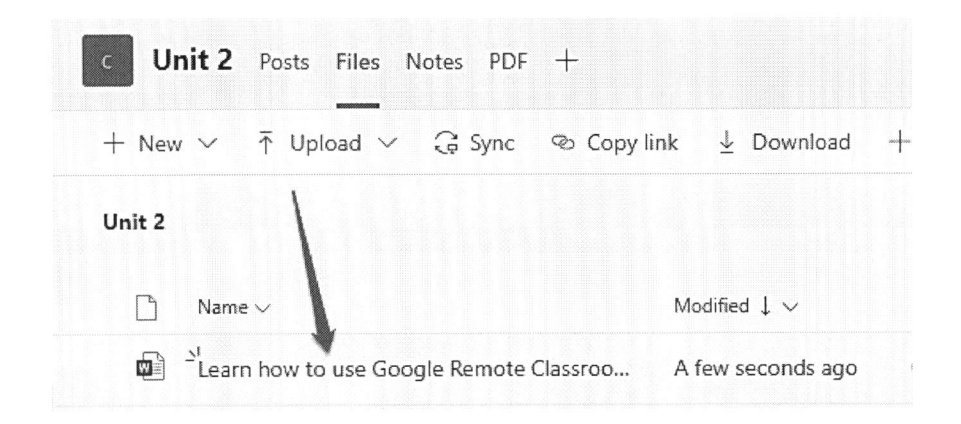

If it is an Office 365 document such as Powerpoint, Excel, or Word, when you click on the file you can go ahead and start making any changes to that document.

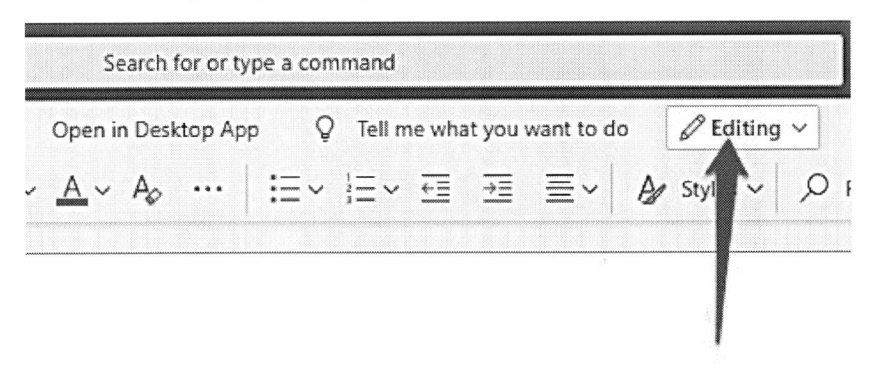

ogle Remote Classroom as a learning management system to train or teach

ılar video conferencing cloud-based virtual meeting platform, which lets you

To start a conversation with your students using the document you just opened, go to the right-hand corner and click on the Conversation button.

57

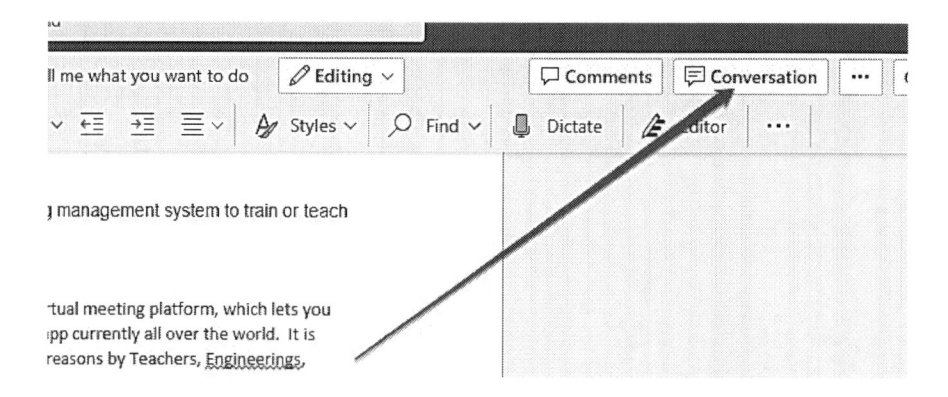

This will open a portion on the Teams window for you to start chatting with your students.

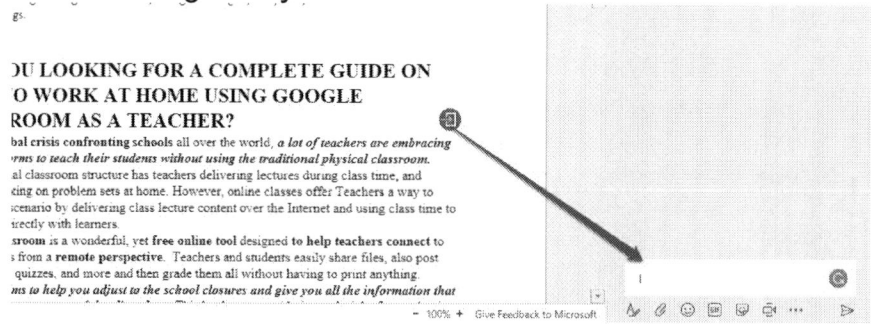

Type in your message and use the arrow button to send.

These conversations are only visible to students who are members of that particular Team.

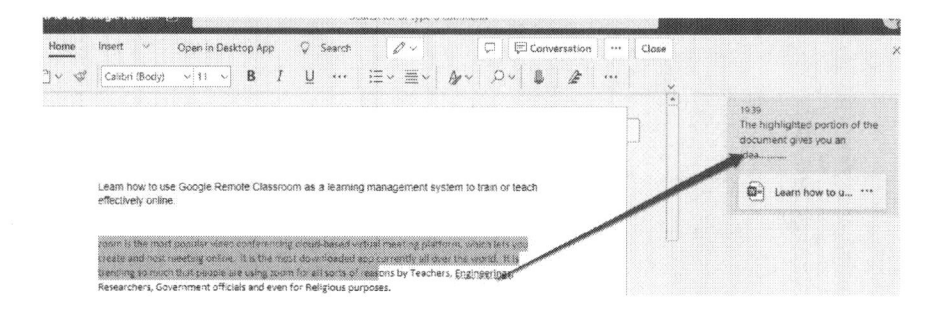

When done, click on the close button to return to the ... window.

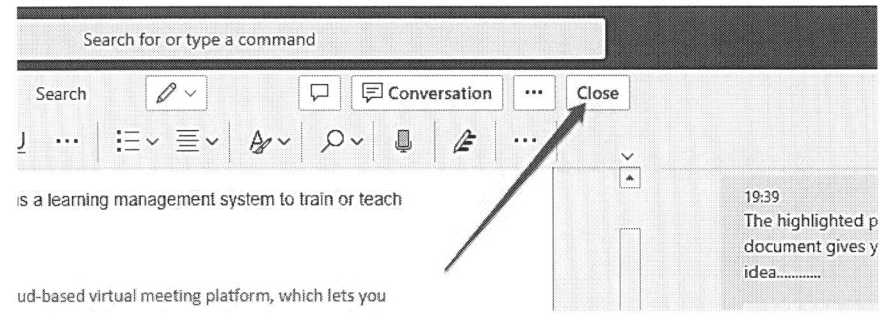

CLASS ASSIGNMENT, CLASS NOTEBOOK, AND FILE SHARING

It is important to have your classroom properly set up and distribute pages to your students for assignments. Microsoft Teams OneNote Class Notebook allows teachers to distribute pages quickly to students in a Microsoft Teams class across several classes. You can distribute a page to your students OneNote class Notebook to enable them to do their homework in the Microsoft Teams assignment tab.

CLASS NOTEBOOK IN TEAMS

Click on the General channel in your teams, locate the Class Notebook tab and click on it.

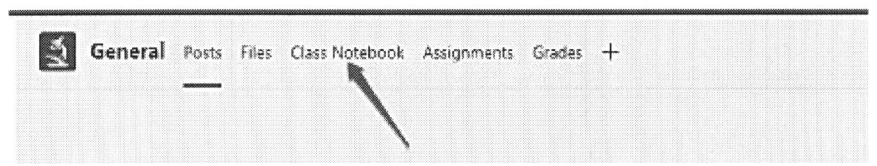

This will be used to create a page that will be distributed to your students in Microsoft Teams.

Next, click on the setup button.

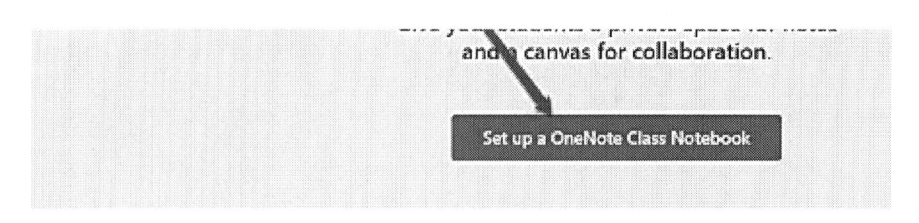

In the next option, select Blank and click on Next, then click on create.

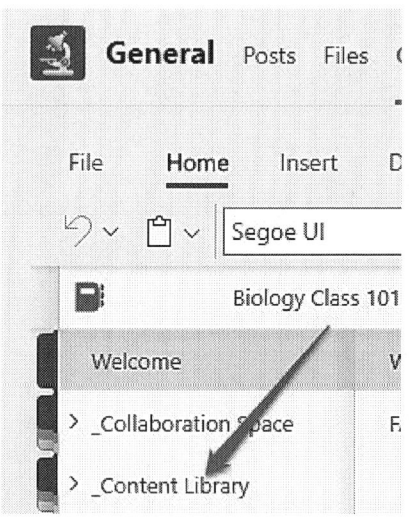

Open your section and locate the *Content Library.*
Click on the Section create button below.

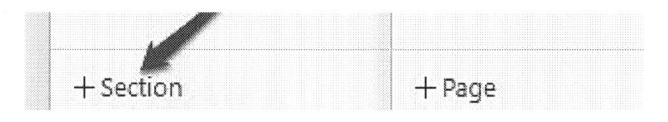

Next, create a section called Assignments.

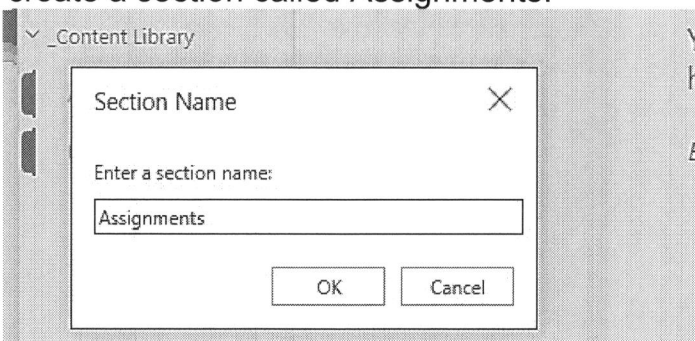

Enter the title of your Assignment Page.

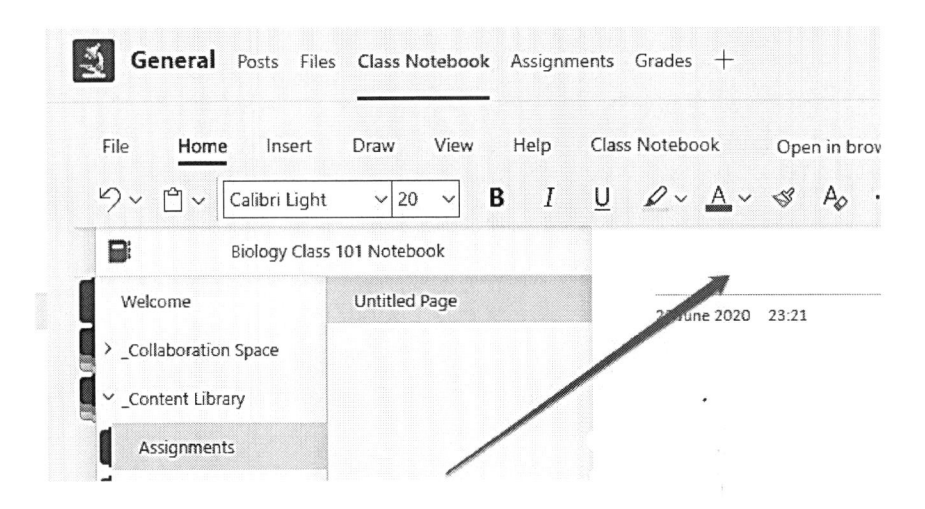

This will automatically rename the page.

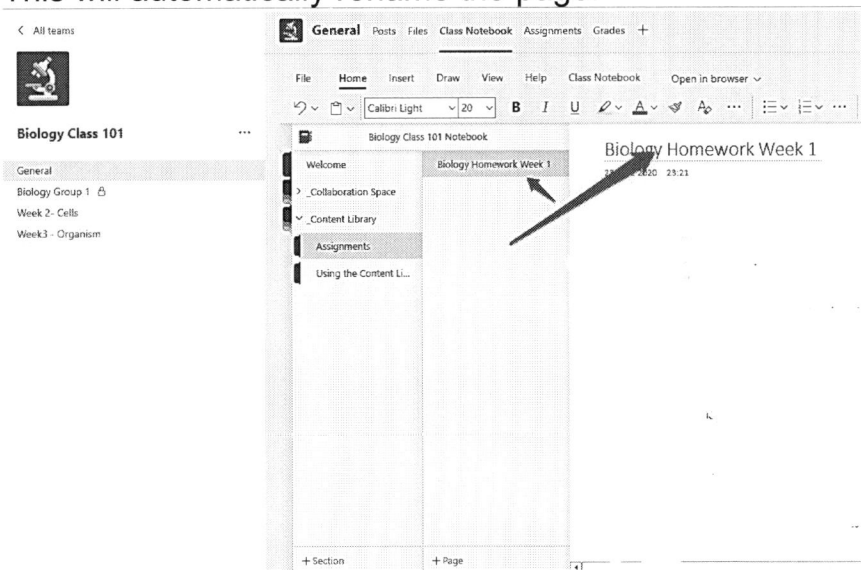

Next, type your questions in the blank space.

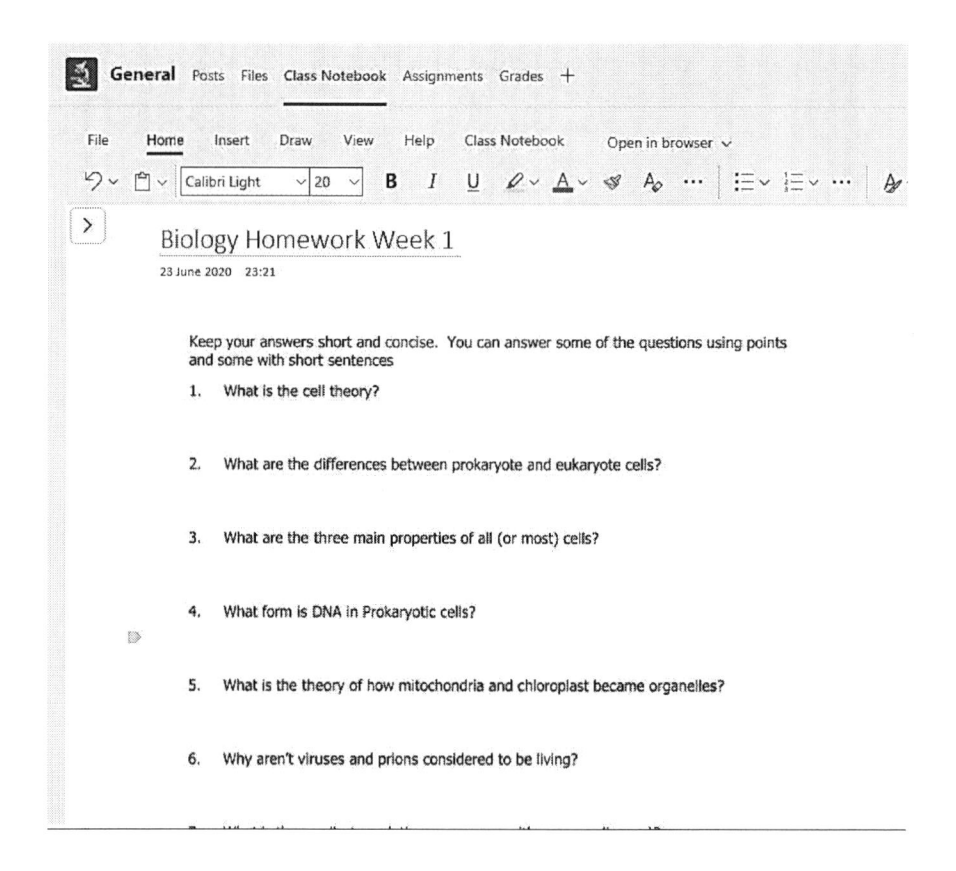

You can also attach a PDF, picture, or link.

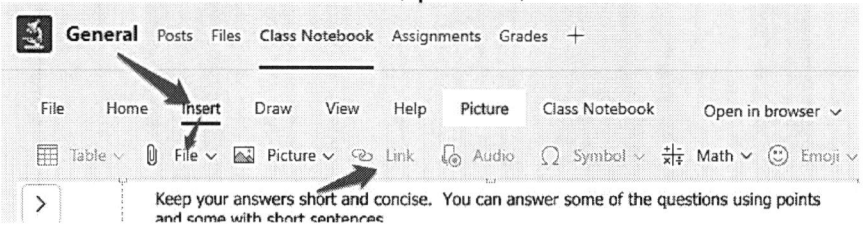

To send your OneNote Class Notebook to your students as an assignment, in your General channel, click on Assignments.

Next, at the bottom of your screen, click on the *Create* button.

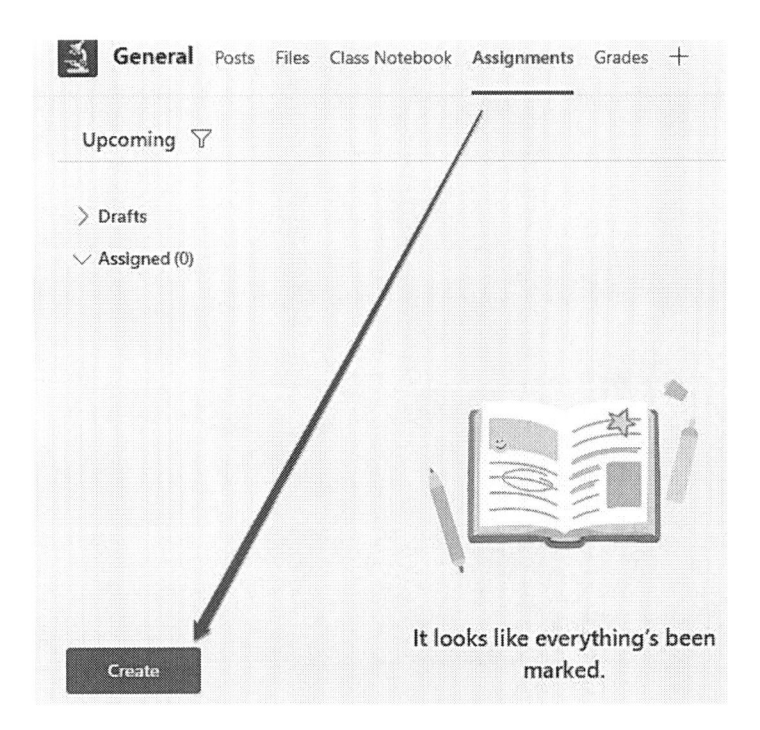

Select assignment from the options provided

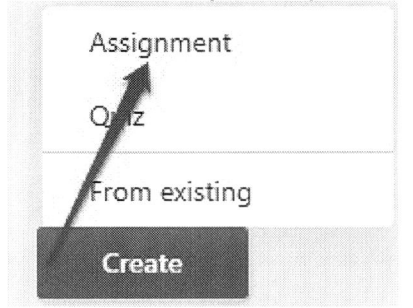

Enter the Title of your assignment and other necessary details where relevant.

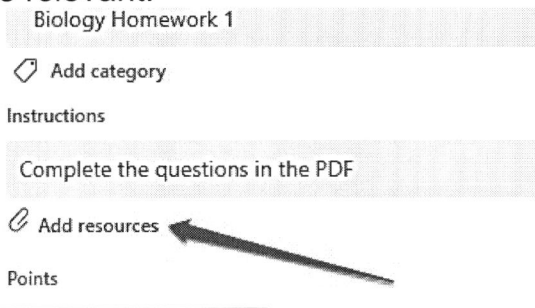

Under resource, you will have to attach the OneNote page you created. Click on the Add Resources button to locate and locate the Assignment. Click on *Attach* to continue.

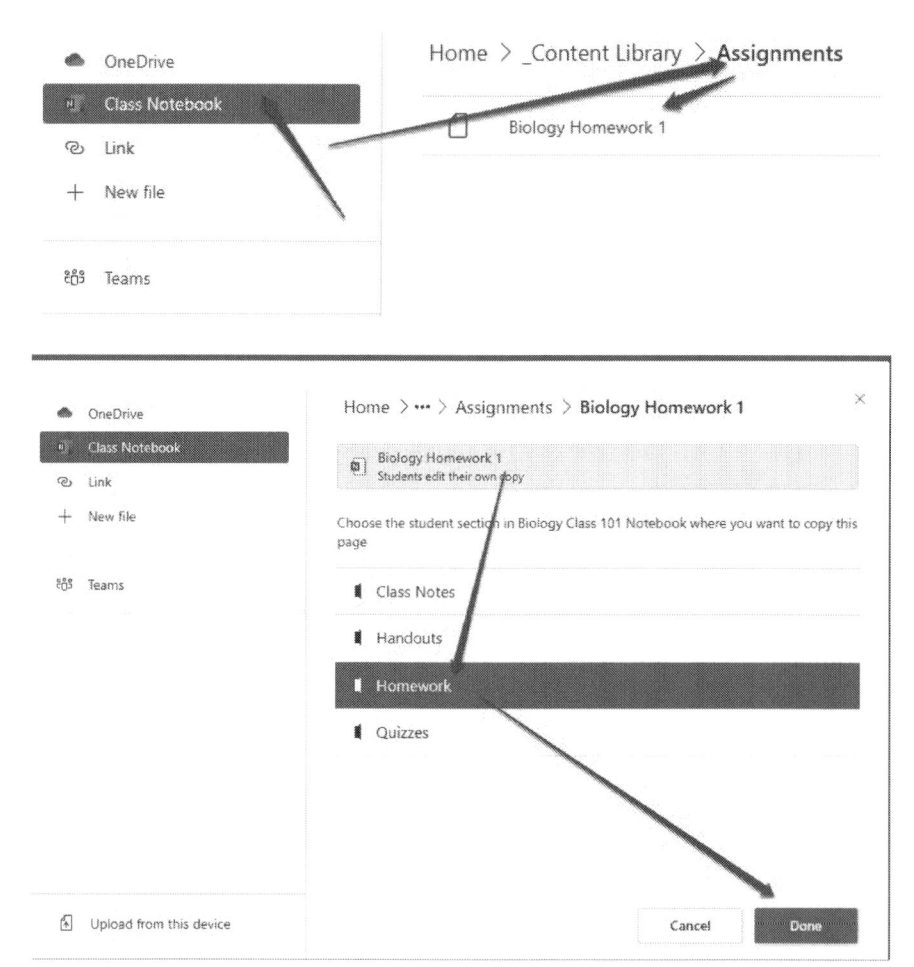

To complete the process, click on the Homework section to have a copy of the page sent to each student.

Title (required)

Biology Homework 1

◇ Add category

Instructions

Complete the questions in the PDF

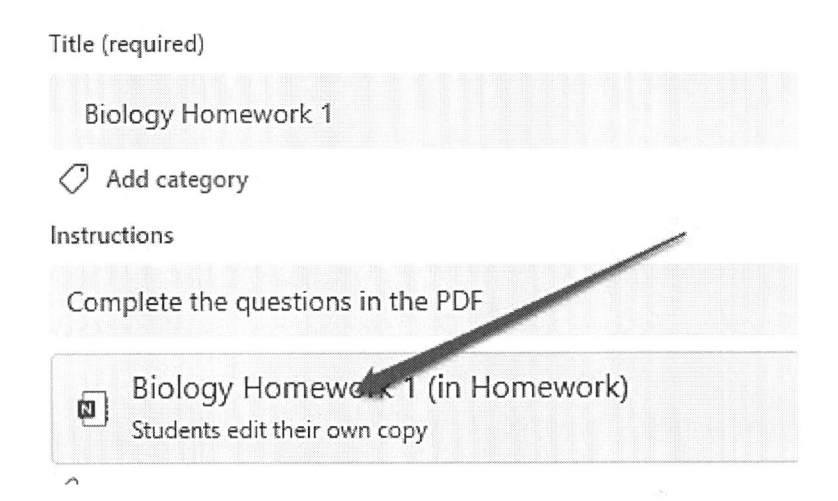

Biology Homework 1 (in Homework)
Students edit their own copy

RUBRIC IN ASSIGNMENTS

During the process of creating an assignment for your students in Microsoft Teams for Education, the rubric section is made optional.

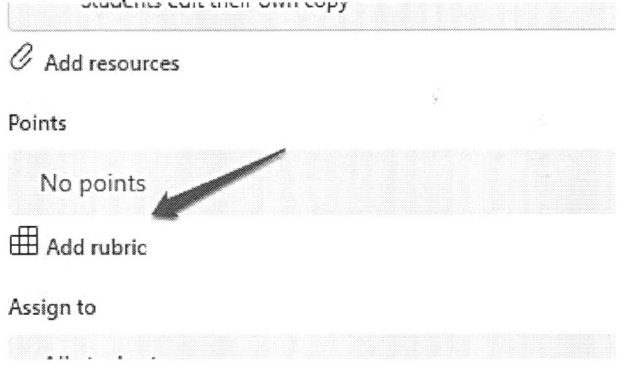

⌂ Add resources

Points

No points

▦ Add rubric

Assign to

Using rubric however gives your students an idea of the grading and helps increase assignment transparency. It tells your students what they need to achieve a certain grade and help them on how to respond to the assignment given to them. Teachers can customize the grading criteria with their rubric to enable the skills-based grading of student's assignments.

When you click on **Add rubric**, add your **Title** (required) and **Description** which is optional.

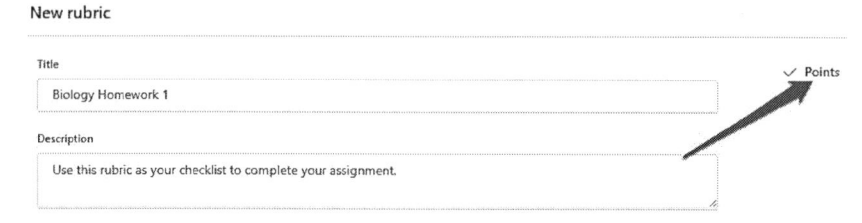

Turn on **Points** to assign a point value to your grading.

CUSTOMIZE YOUR GRADING CRITERIA FOR RUBRIC

The Excellent, Good, Fair and Poor defaults can be edited to match your assignment grading strategy.

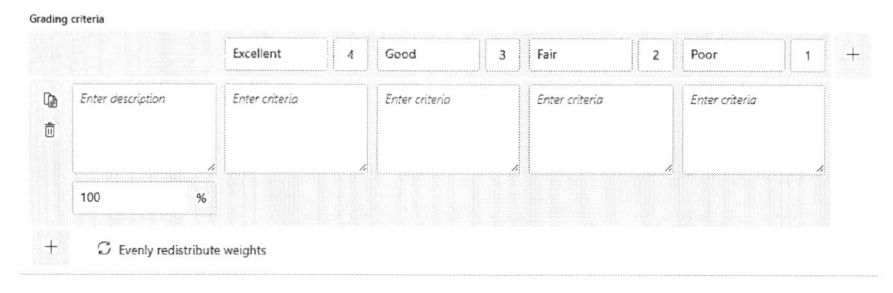

Use the plus signs to add new columns and rows to your criteria.

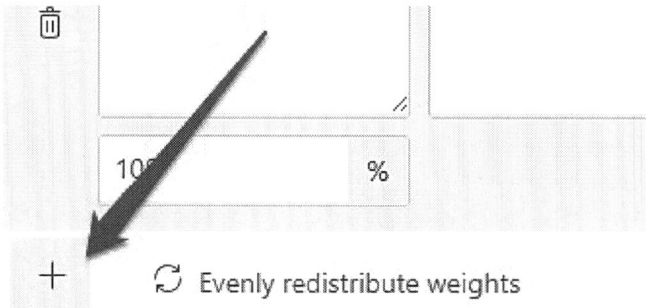

Use the copy icon by your left to duplicate a row or column.

If you wish to delete a row or column, click on the garbage icon.

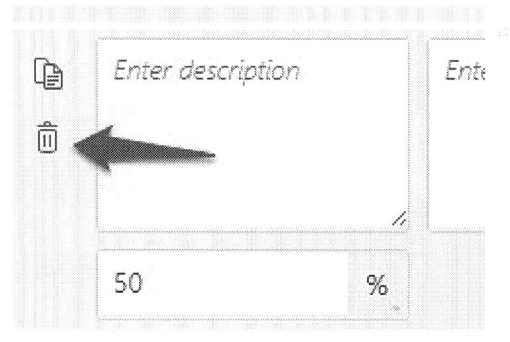

When it is time to weigh your criteria, enter a percentage of 100 to weight some criteria heavier than others, or use the ***Evenly distribute weight*** to spread them across the number of rows.

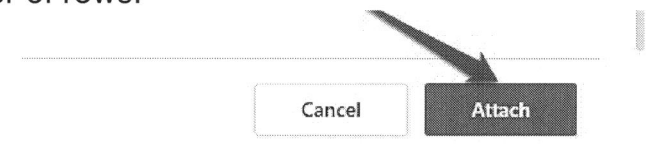

When done, click on the ***Attach*** button to complete the process.

Next, you have the *Assign to*, used to decide which of the ***Teams*** you want to assign the assignment to. If you have more than one Team, you will need to choose the one you want to send the assignment.

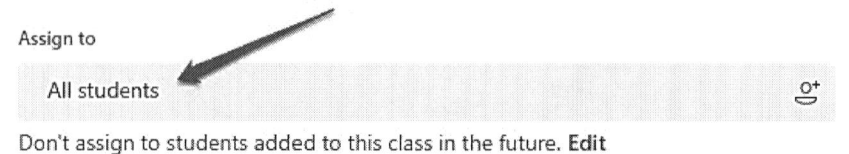

Assign to

All students

Don't assign to students added to this class in the future. **Edit**

Set the date in which you want your students to return the assignment.

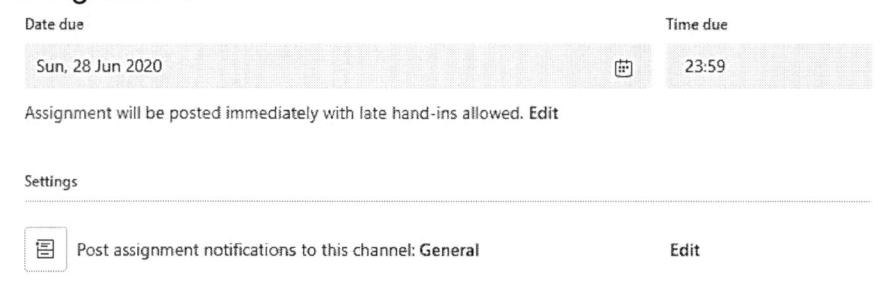

Date due	Time due
Sun, 28 Jun 2020	23:59

Assignment will be posted immediately with late hand-ins allowed. **Edit**

Settings

Post assignment notifications to this channel: **General**   Edit

Click on the *Assign* button to complete the process.

Saved: 24 Jun, 00:04   Discard   Save   **Assign**

LESSON SEVEN

VIDEO CONFERENCING

Microsoft Teams for Education also allows teachers and students to have video discussion on their laptop or mobile device.

AD-HOC MEETINGS

As a teacher, you can have a ***ad-hoc meeting*** with your students using the meet now button within a channel.

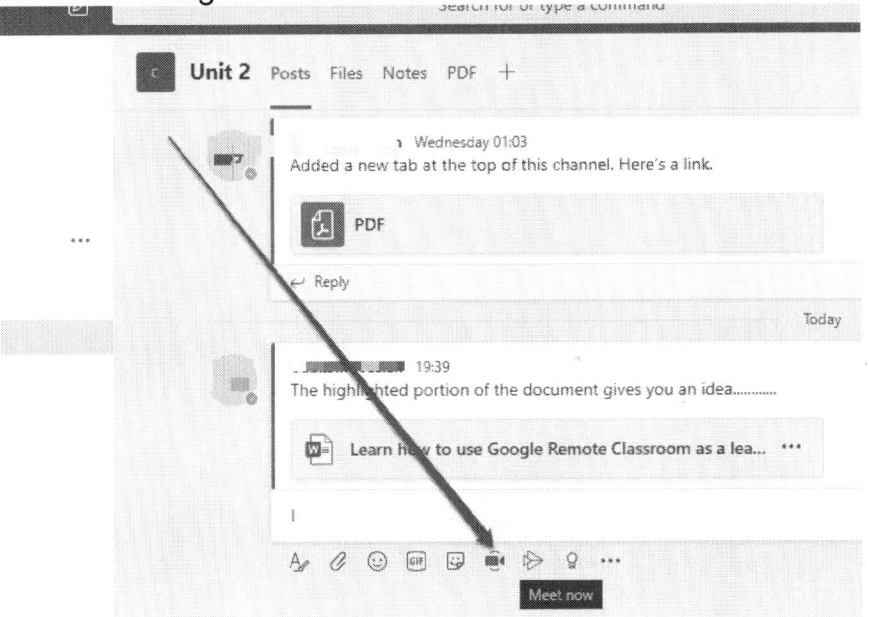

The ad-hoc meetings get all members of your Teams together in a video conversation. It is a quick way to give further explanation on a subject using video or your computer screen.

Next, add a subject of discussion to help your student have an idea of the purpose of the instant meeting and click on the meet now button to start the meeting.

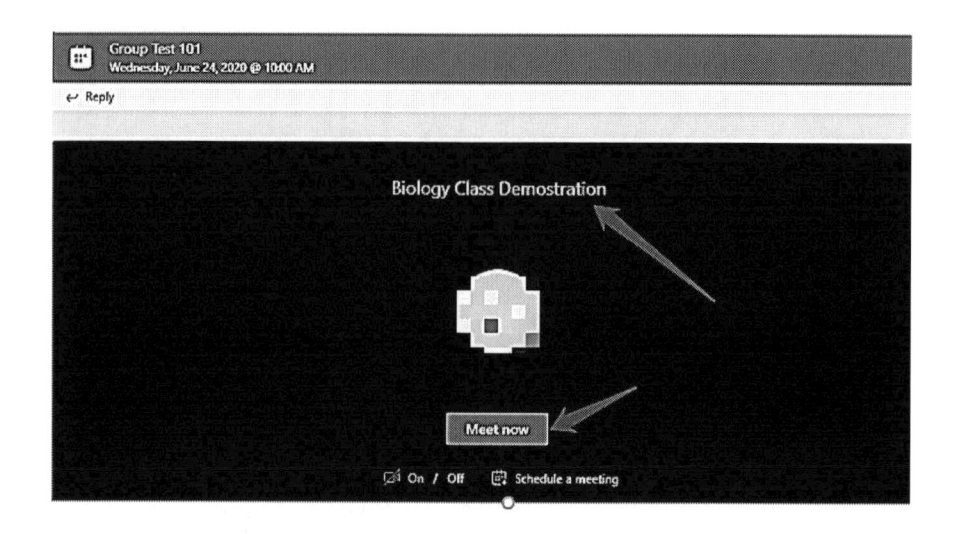

PRIVATE OR GROUP MEETINGS

The other type of video conferencing is a **Private or Group meeting**, in which there is a 1-on-1 conversations with a specific group of students. Private or group meetings won't appear in any of your channel conversations.

To start a private meeting, click on the Call tab and then click on the **New chat** button beside the search bar.

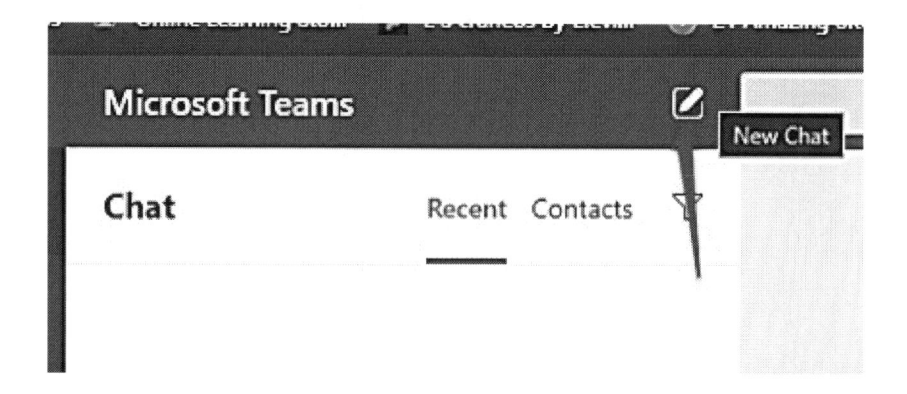

Next, enter the names of the students you want to have a private or group meeting with.

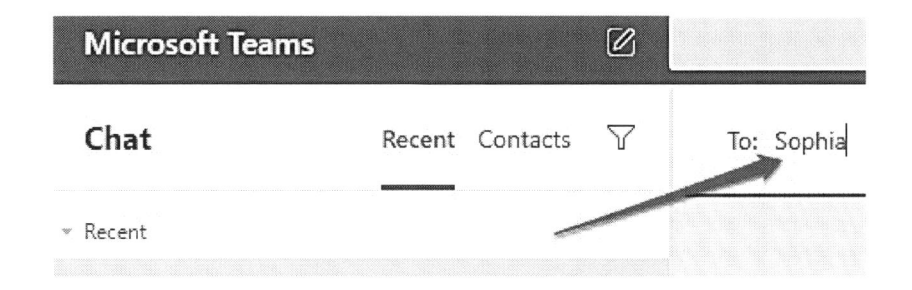

![Microsoft Teams Chat screenshot showing "To: Sophia"]

Next, on the top right corner of your window, click on the video call icon to start a video conversation.

![Video call and phone call icons]

CHANNEL MEETINGS

A Channel meeting is one held with an entire team or students. This means a schedule for such meetings can be set and students will be sent an alert when it is time to join the meeting on their own interface.

Click on the Calendar tab on the navigation bar.

![Navigation bar showing Assignments, Calendar, and Calls icons]

Next, on the top right corner of your screen, click on the **New Meeting** button.

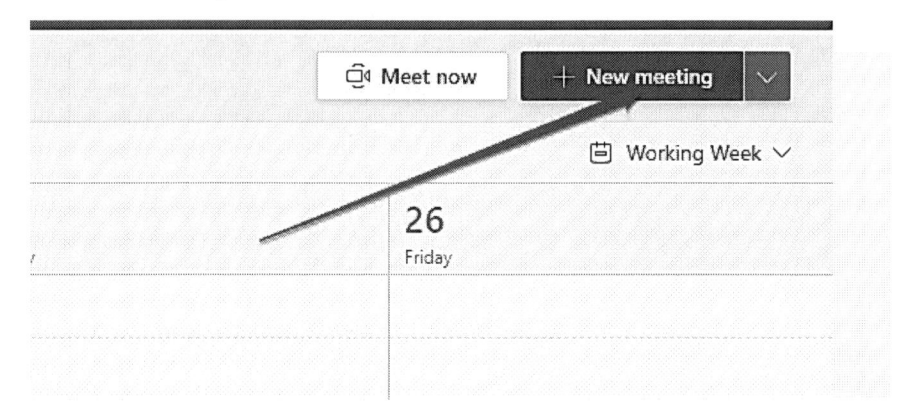

This process is the same with web and desktop applications.

Next give your meeting a title, set the date and time, including the channel you which to hold the meeting. Only members who have access to the channel you choose will be able to join the meeting.

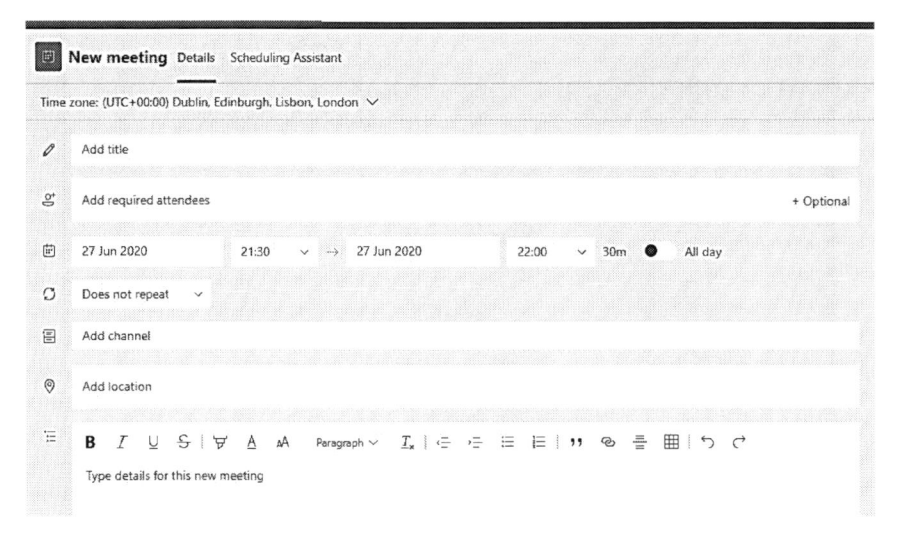

You can also add a non-teams member to your meeting.

72

HOW TO INVITE A NON-TEAM MEMBER TO A MEETING

When creating a New meeting schedule in your Teams, where you have the *Add required attendances*, you can add people who are not members of your teams. Such persons can be parents or co-teachers.

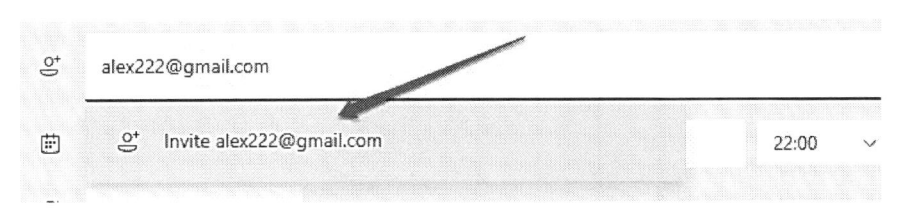

Since they are not members of your teams, when you enter their email address, you will need to manually click on the *invite* to confirm the invitation. When done click on the **Save** button to close the scheduling form and sends the invite to those invited.

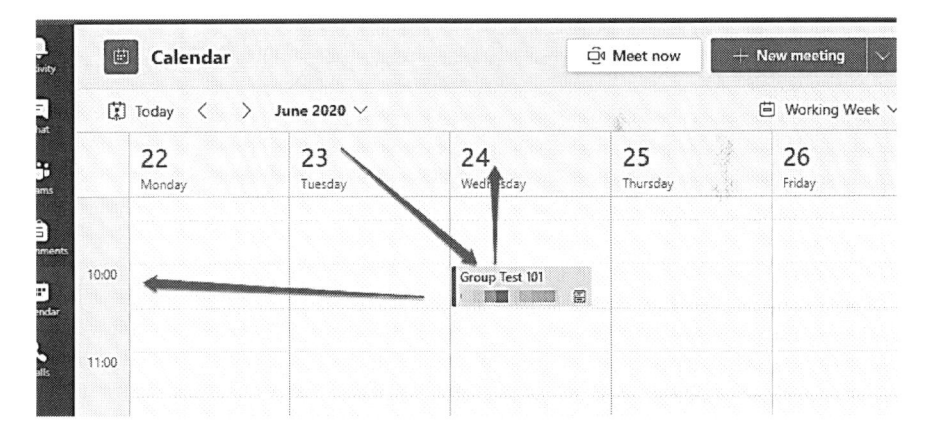

The Microsoft Exchange calendar will show a **Join** button five minutes before a meeting starts.

SETTING MEETING OPTIONS

The meeting options settings allow teachers to set meeting features to have full control when your meeting starts. When scheduling a meeting or going back to edit your meetings, locate and click the meeting options button to open a different window.

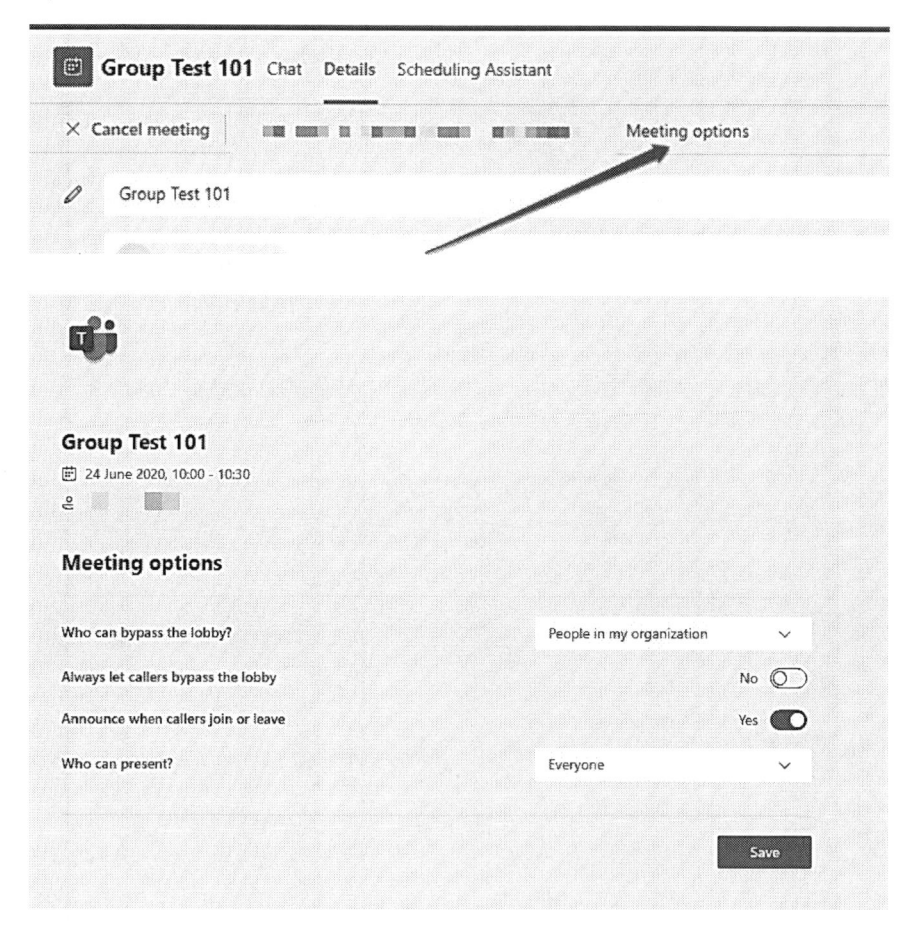

Who can bypass the lobby allow people calling in by phone to join your meeting without the need to wait for you to admit them.

The who can present setting determine who you want to be a presenter.

HOW TO SET A PRESENTER IN A TEAM MEETING

By default when teachers add students to a Teams Meeting they join as presenters. This poses an issue since such students are allowed to mute each other, remove each other from a meeting, and stop meeting recording. Using the meeting options in Microsoft Teams will help decide who can present and the right each member has.

Go to the Calendar tab and click on the meeting you might have scheduled earlier, and click on *meeting options*.

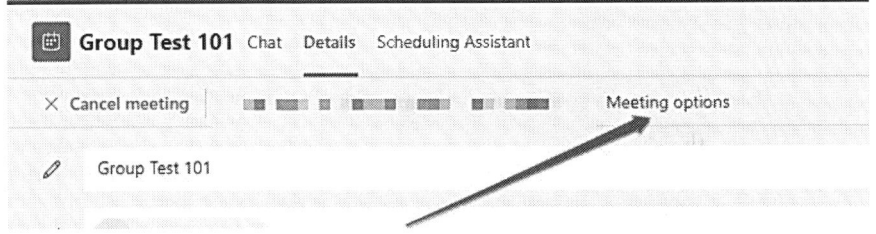

Use the dropdown menu to choose who you want to be a Presenter.

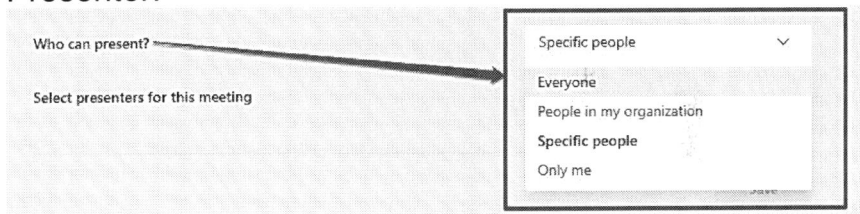

When done, click on the **Save** button to complete the process.

A designated presenter will have full control over your meeting. A presenter can mute or kick students out of a meeting.

JOINING A SCHEDULED MEETING

The Microsoft teams calendar tab is automatically synced to your Exchange calendar. Calendar reminds you of when a meeting will begin and allow you to review and prepare.

To view all your scheduled meetings, click on the **Calendar Menu.**

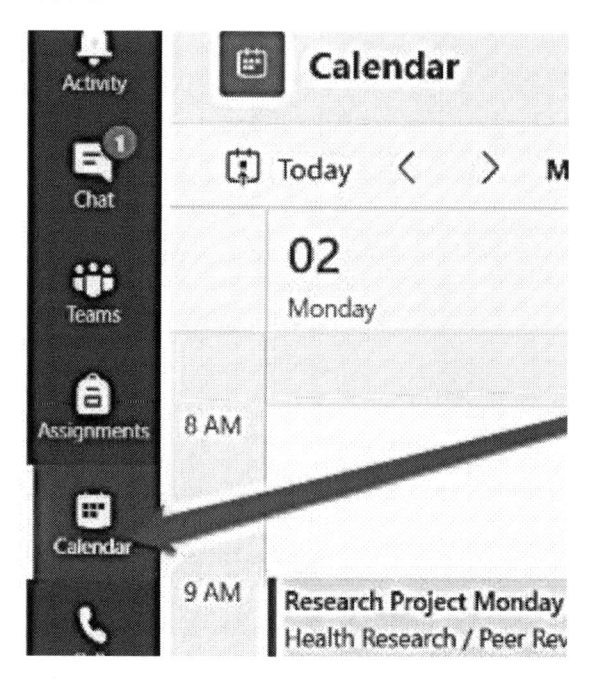

Next, select the scheduled meeting and click on the join button.

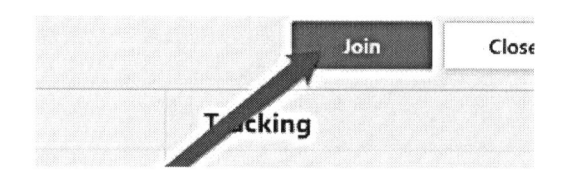

STATING A PRIVATE MEETING

Click on the calendar bar on the Navigation tab and then click on the Meet Now button to start a private meeting.

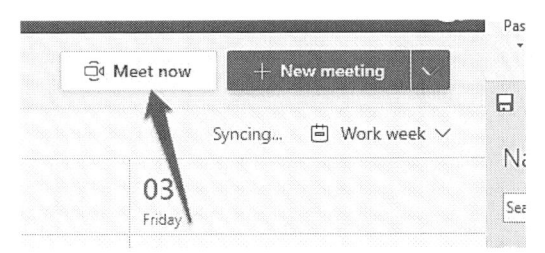

Next, enter your name in the box provided.

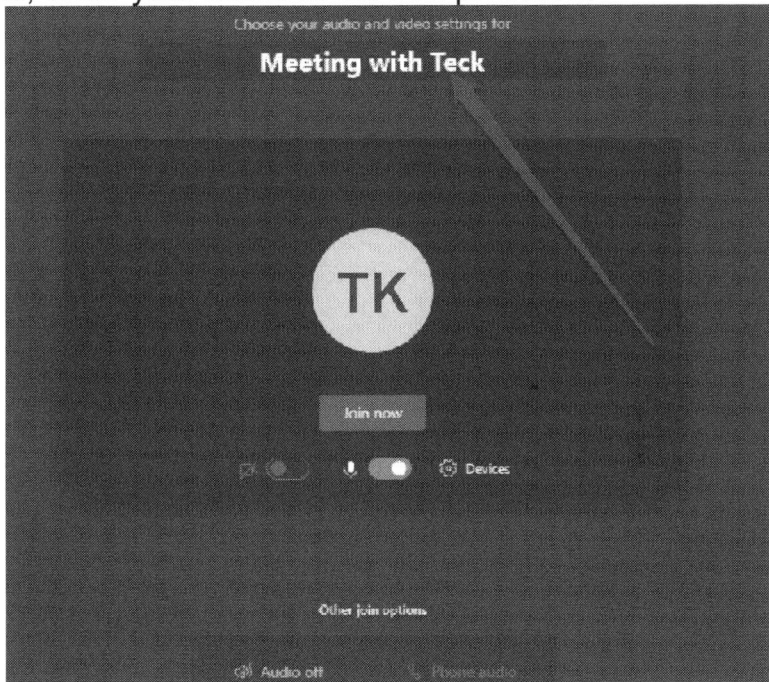

Click on the Join Now button to start the meeting.

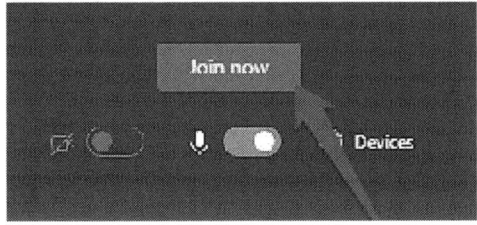

Once your meeting has started, you will be asked to invite people to join your private meeting.

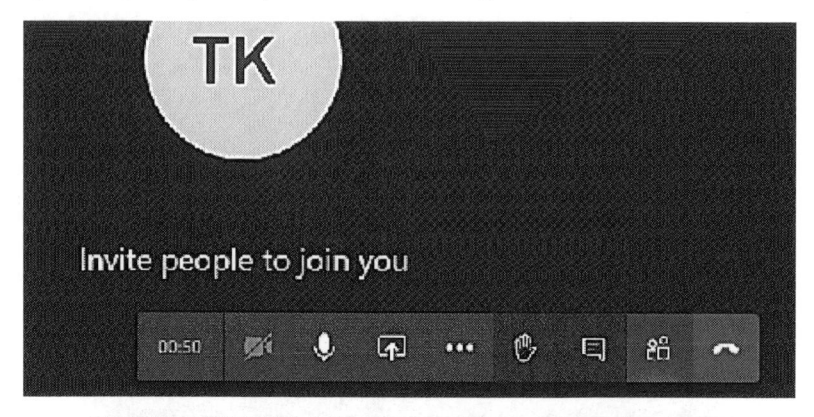

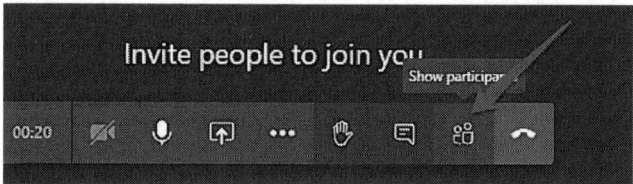

To invite your students to a private meeting, click on the *show participants* button.

On the right corner of your screen, where you have the people panel, click inside the **invite box** and enter the name or email address of students you want to add to your private meeting.

TEAMS MEETING CONTROLS

The controls feature you can use while participating in a Microsoft Teams meeting can be found inside the bottom portion of the meeting video window. Although, some advanced features are only available with full functionality when joining a Teams meeting on desktop.

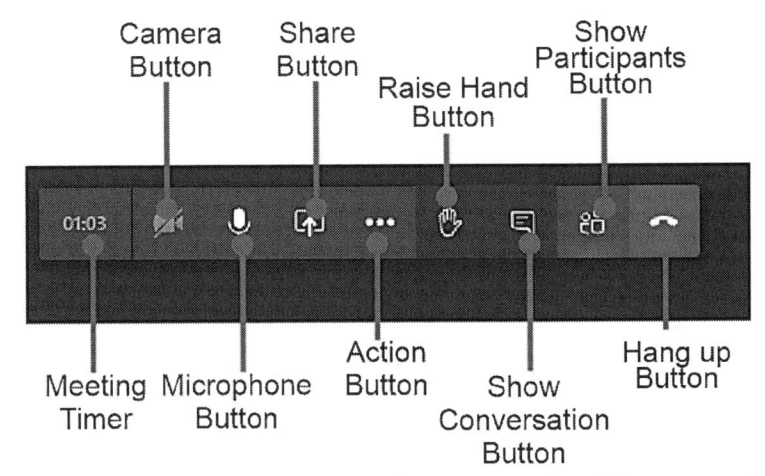

```
Camera    Share              Show
Button    Button          Participants
                Raise Hand   Button
                  Button
```

```
          Action         Hang up
Meeting Microphone Button  Show    Button
Timer   Button         Conversation
                         Button
```

- **Meeting Timer** displays the amount of time you have spent in the meeting.
- **Camera button** turns your camera on or off. If your camera is off, the camera icon will have a slash through it.
- **Microphone button** mutes or unmutes your microphone. If your microphone is muted, the microphone icon will have a slash through it.
- **Share button** opens a panel with options for sharing your device screen, a specific window, PowerPoint files, or Microsoft Whiteboard. Check the system audio box if you want to share audio from an application, then click on an item to share it with meeting participants. While you are sharing, you can click on the share button again to stop sharing.
- **More Actions button** opens a menu of additional Teams actions and features. Among the options listed in this menu are options for accessing device settings, entering full-screen mode, and starting or stopping a meeting recording.
- **Raise Your Hand button** alerts the presenter(s) that you have something to contribute while a meeting is going on without interrupting the ongoing conversation. Other participants will be able to see an icon next to

your name that indicates you have your hand raised. This icon shows up in both the video window and the People panel.
- **Show Conversation button** opens the Meeting chat panel on the right side of the meeting window and chat with meeting participants.
- **Show Participants button** opens the People panel on the right side of the meeting window and views a list of meeting attendees. As a teacher who is also an organizer or a Presenter, you may admit any guests waiting in the meeting lobby by clicking the checkmark next to their name.
- **Hang Up button** allows you to leave the meeting. Other participants will be able to continue without you. If you would like to end the meeting for all participants, click on More Actions > End Meeting.

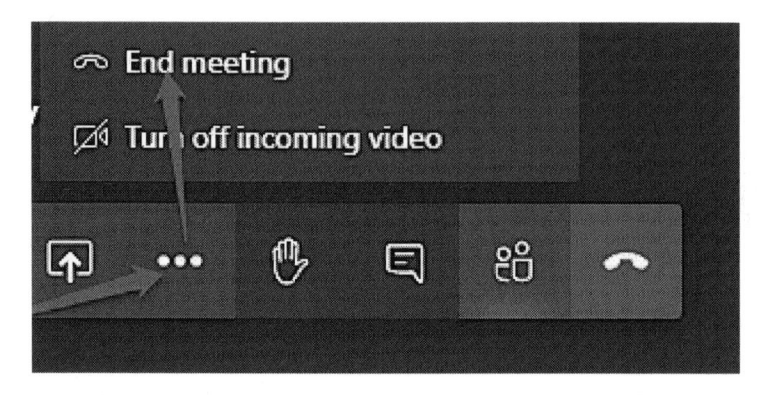

TEAMS MEETINGS BOMBING

Teams bombing can be avoided using the attendee and presenter roles. If you make your students attendee, they can not mute others or remove each other from a meeting. They can't also share their screens. During a meeting, you can click on the Show participants icon on your meeting controls to view participants.

Next, click on the *Manage permission* icon on the People panel.

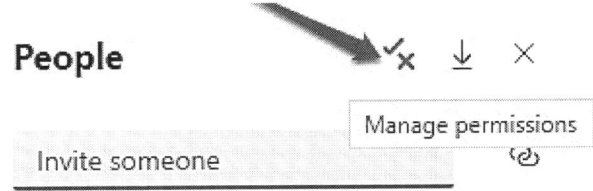

This will open a separate tab on your browser for the Meeting options settings.

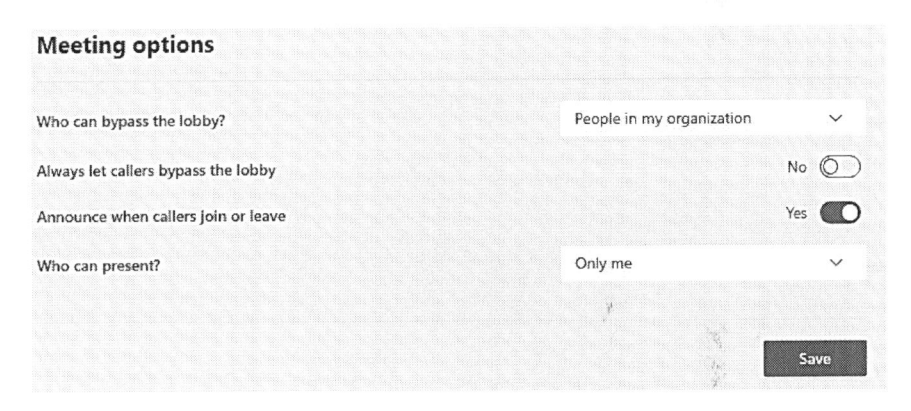

Set **presenter** to **Only me**, which makes the teacher the sole **presenter.** For those who can **bypass the lobby**, set it to **People in my organization**, which is similar to Zoom waiting room settings to prevent anonymous participants.

Disable callers bypass to lobby. This will help prevent Teams bombing. When done click on the **Save** button to complete the process.

RECORDING YOUR MEETINGS

Record your meetings in Microsoft Teams to capture video, audio, and screen sharing activity. The recording takes place in the cloud and is saved to Microsoft Stream, so you can share it securely with your students.

If you are wondering how to record Microsoft Teams meeting, here is everything you need to know. Once your meeting has started, go to the meeting controls and click on the *Action button*.

Now click on *Start Recording*.

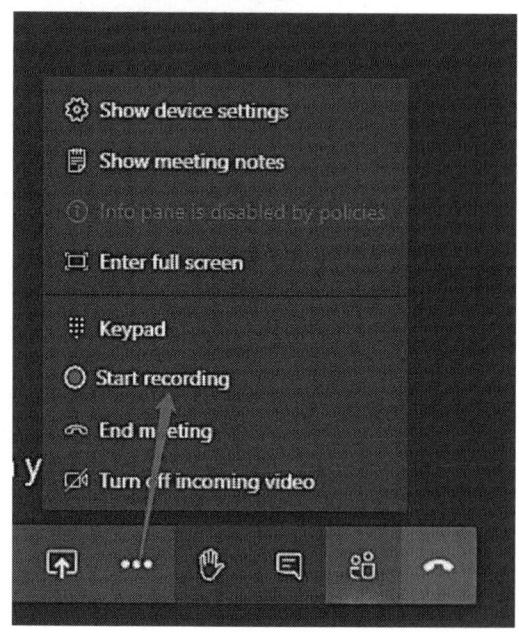

Everyone in the meeting will be notified that the recording has started. Your meeting notification is also posted to the chat history.

Microsoft teams do not allow multiple recordings of the same meeting simultaneously.

To stop recording a meeting, go to the meeting controls and click on the Action button, and click on "**Stop recording**."

Once you click on Stop recording, the record will be processed and then saved to Microsoft Stream. An email will be sent to you from Microsoft Stream when the recording is available and also appears in the meeting chat.

SETTING A CUSTOM BACKGROUND
An attractive background is important when conducting a video conference. Your background is an essential element that should not distract your participants. You can change your background to something alluring in teams.

Once you start your meeting, click on the **Action panel**, and select ***Show background effects***

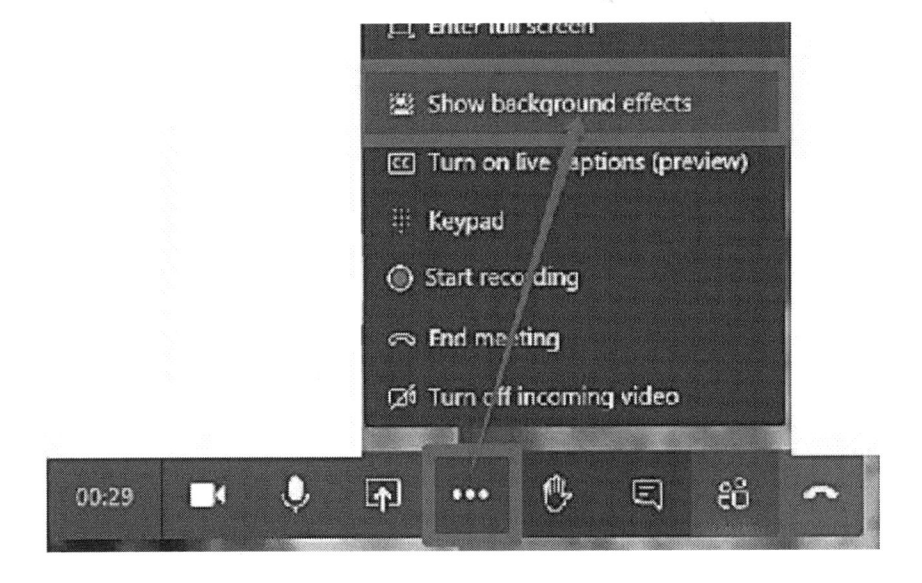

This will bring display a sidebar with some alternative background options. You can use stock photos from Microsoft's extensive list.

Click on the *Upload* or *Use* button to start using a Microsoft custom background for your video call.

HOW TO BLUR YOUR MICROSOFT TEAMS BACKGROUND

Click on your audio and video settings screen when you join a meeting. Choose the Action button and select *Show background effects*. Tap on *Blur* to blur your background. You will see a preview of the background to see how it looks like before you apply it.

TEAMS WHITEBOARD SHARING

Whiteboard is extremely usable for classwork collaboration within Microsoft Teams. Teams allow teachers to create whiteboard, share it, and chat while collaborating. Whiteboard on Team's desktop or web platform can be accessed by clicking on the share button, and only accessible in a team's channel during a visual meeting.

Once you click on the Sharing button, and it will prompt you to select from your current desktop, active windows, any PowerPoint slides, browse files from PC/Mac, other Teams channel, or your OneDrive. Also included is the Whiteboard with two options to choose from; Microsoft Whiteboard or Freehand by InVision.

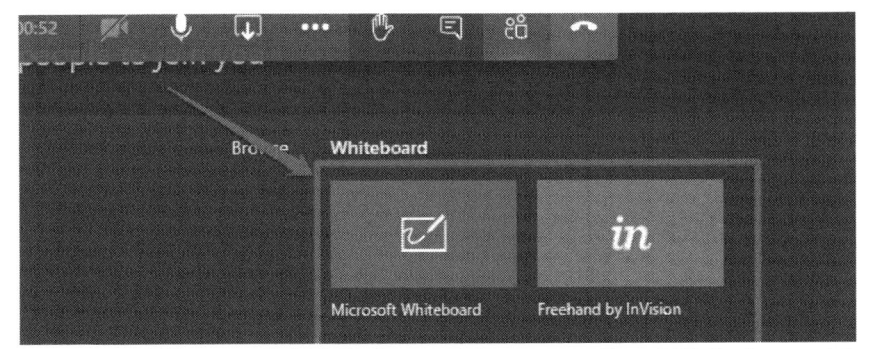

Click on Microsoft Whiteboard to open the Whiteboard to start using it.

MICROSOFT WHITEBOARD DRAWING FEATURES

Microsoft Whiteboard offers a lot of drawing options while using the Whiteboard. Teachers can use the standard Pen tool in Black, Red, Green, and Blue, color for your illustrations.

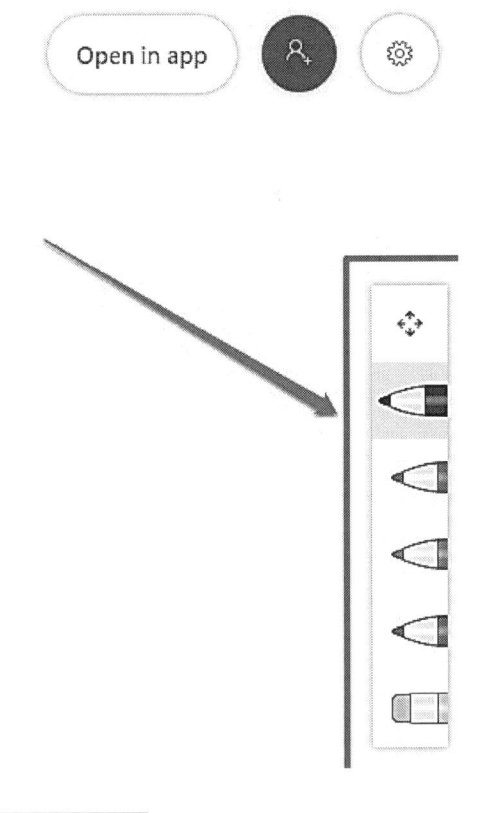

The eraser tool allows you to remove portions from the Whiteboard.

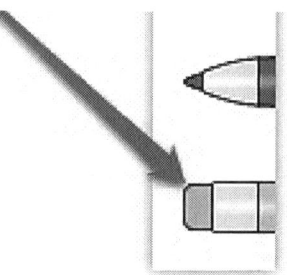

The move tool is used to move the Whiteboard or keep the Whiteboard at a fixed section.

HOW TO EXPORT A WHITEBOARD CONTENT
If you wish to save the content of your Whiteboard as an image on your computer, tap on the Settings icon at the top right corner, and select Export image in SVG format.

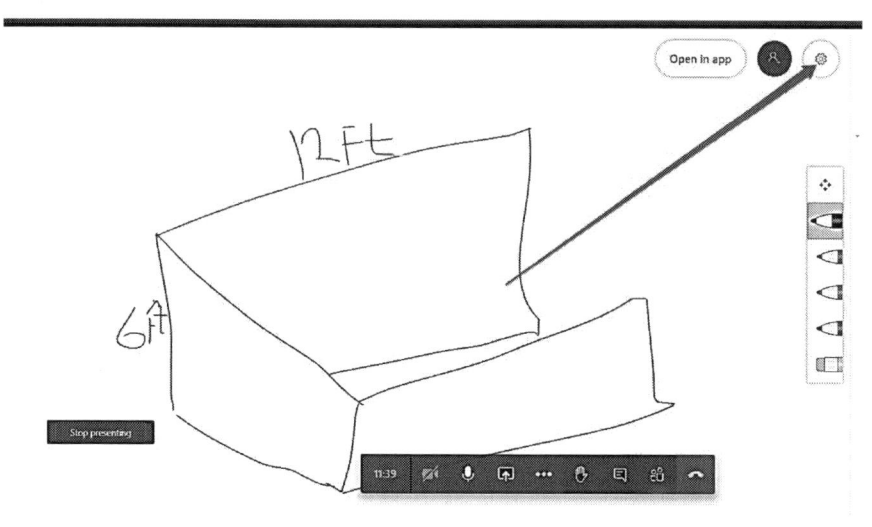

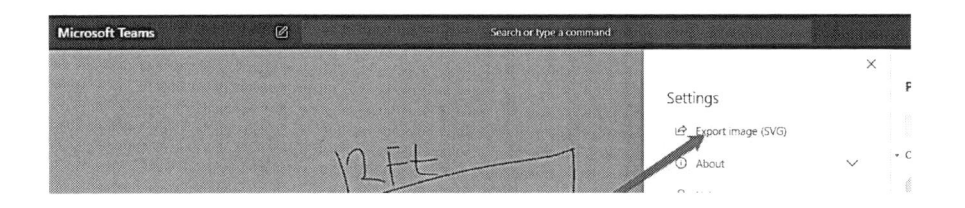

HOW TO SHARE WHITEBOARD AND CHAT

During screen sharing, you can also ask students to join the stream. Click on the Share button at the top left corner, and it will generate a sharing link.

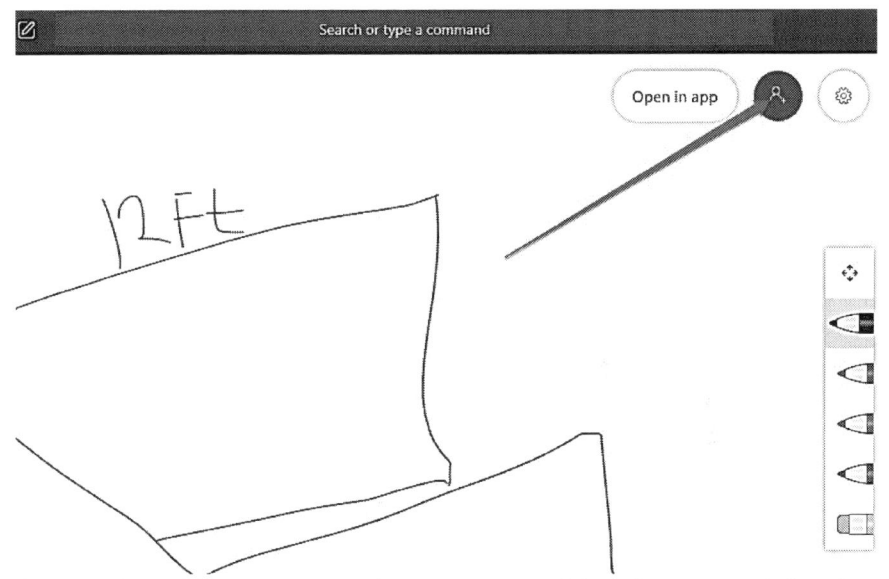

Share it with your students to enable them to join the session.

While using the Whiteboard, you can also click on the Chat button to chat with your students.

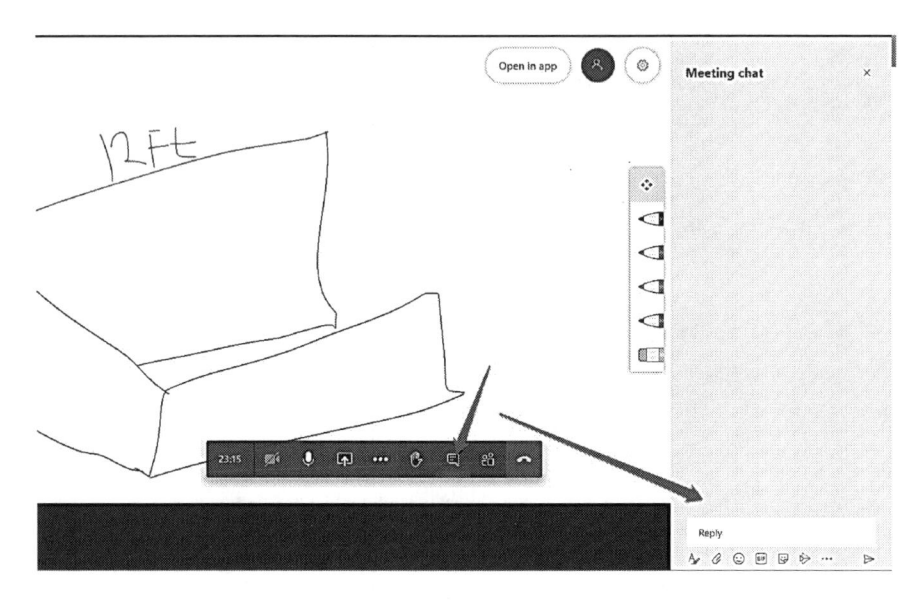

The chat button opens the side window within the Whiteboard and allows you to chat with your students. This way, you can communicate live with your students and they can discuss among themselves during whiteboard screen sharing. When the meetings end, you can see all the chat history with the Meeting name on the Channel.

CLASS MEETING ATTENDANCE

As a teacher, if you wish to have a list of students that attended your meeting, click on the *Show Participant* button, then click on the download attendance icon.

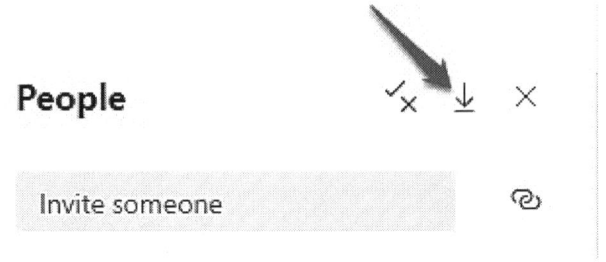

This will download an excel sheet of all participants in a particular meeting.

HOW TO STOP EMAIL NOTIFICATIONS

Click on your profile picture, then select *Settings, next* click on *Notifications*.

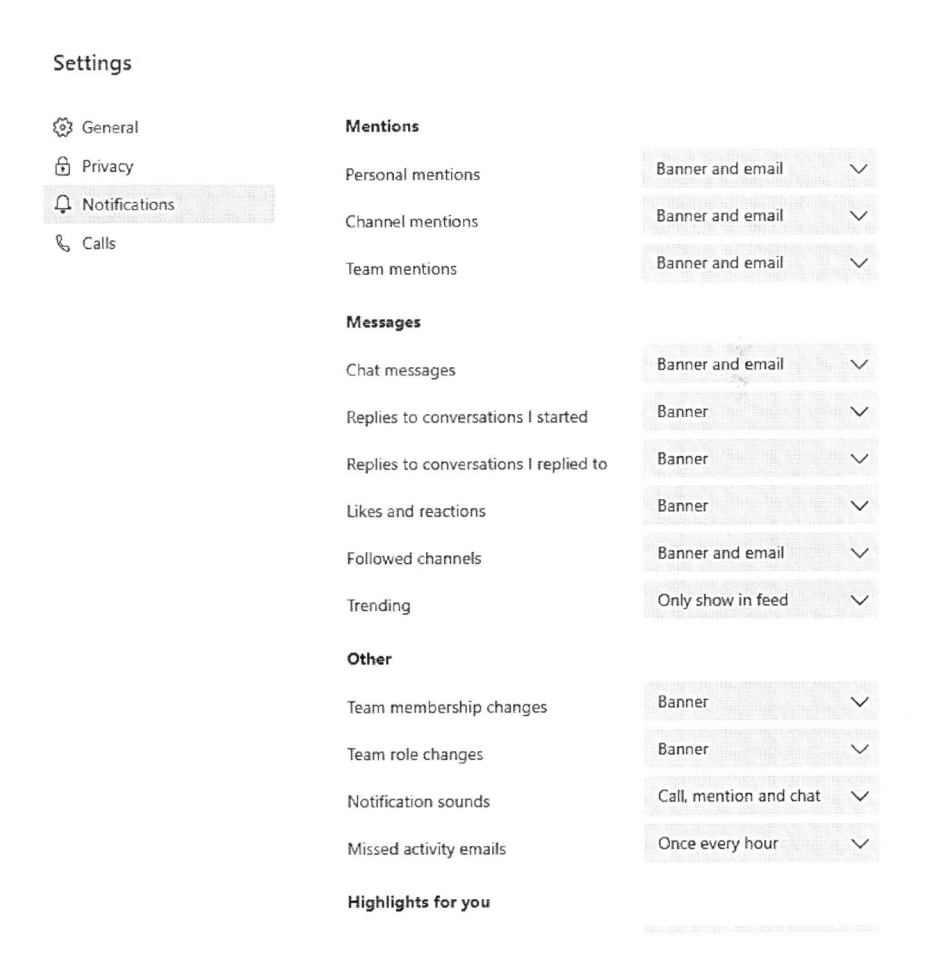

Settings		
⚙ General	**Mentions**	
🔒 Privacy	Personal mentions	Banner and email
🔔 Notifications	Channel mentions	Banner and email
📞 Calls	Team mentions	Banner and email
	Messages	
	Chat messages	Banner and email
	Replies to conversations I started	Banner
	Replies to conversations I replied to	Banner
	Likes and reactions	Banner
	Followed channels	Banner and email
	Trending	Only show in feed
	Other	
	Team membership changes	Banner
	Team role changes	Banner
	Notification sounds	Call, mention and chat
	Missed activity emails	Once every hour
	Highlights for you	

Now you can set the type of notifications you need for each type of activity on Teams. If you don't want any emails, ensure all activity types are set to *otherwise*.

89

LESSON EIGHT

ADVANCED TIPS AND TRICK

HOW TO MANAGE NOTIFICATIONS IN TEAMS

There are several ways to access and manage notifications. To additionally customize your team's notification settings, click on your profile picture at the top-right corner of Teams, select *Settings*, and click on *Notifications*.

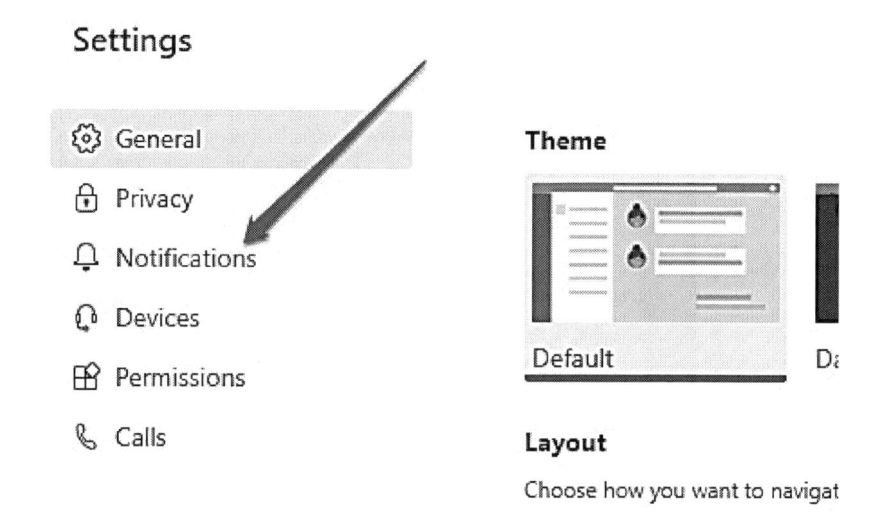

You can modify what notifications you want and where to receive your notifications.

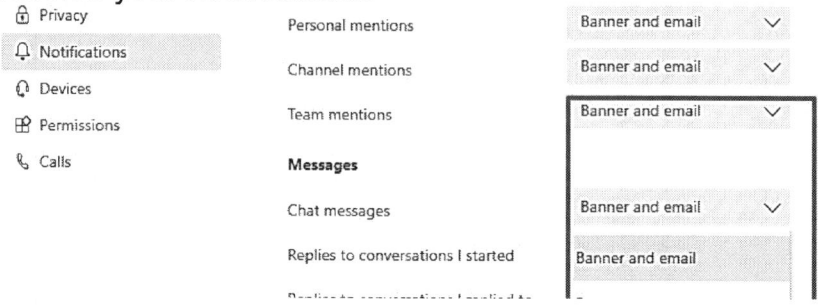

NOTIFICATION PRIORITY SET UP

Modifying the Priority access in Teams will block unimportant notifications during class presentations and meetings. Only vital notification during your presentation can come in, so you can decide to enable this option if you need it by following these steps;

With the client app running, click on your user profile picture, and click on Settings. Click on the Privacy tab, and select Manage Priority Access.

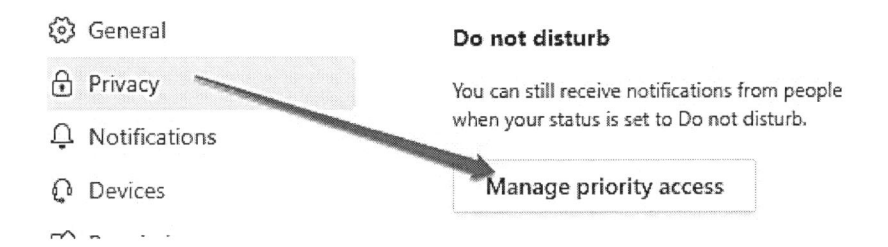

Next, click and *Add Students* whose notifications you want to see.

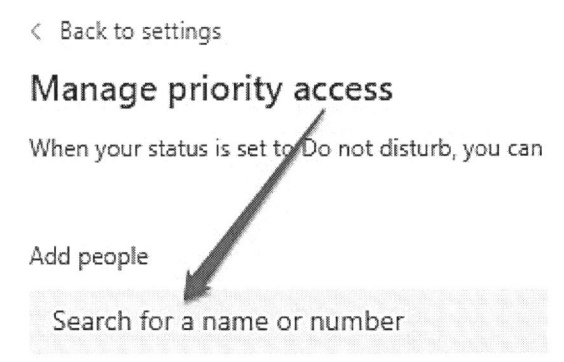

DO NOT DISTURB AND

Distractions such as unnecessary notifications during an online class can mess up your presentation.

Click on your profile picture and change the Availability option to Do not disturb.

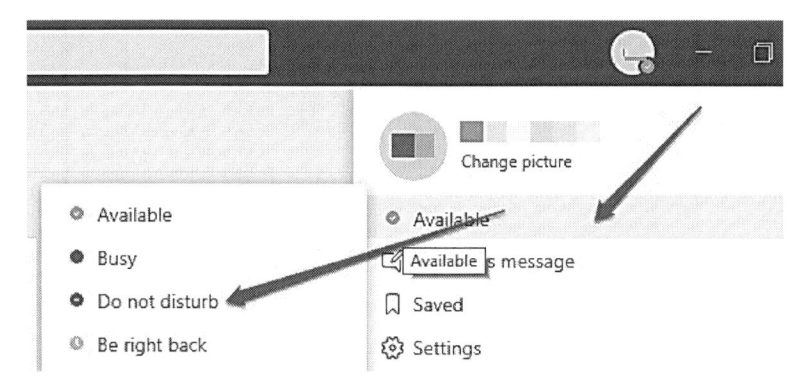

HOW TO ENABLE DARK MODE

If your eyes are sensitive to your computer or device screen, using Dark mode will help reduce the strains. Microsoft Teams for Education has a dark mode feature you can turn on. On the web platform or desktop client apps: Click on your profile picture in the top right corner of the screen and click on *Settings*.

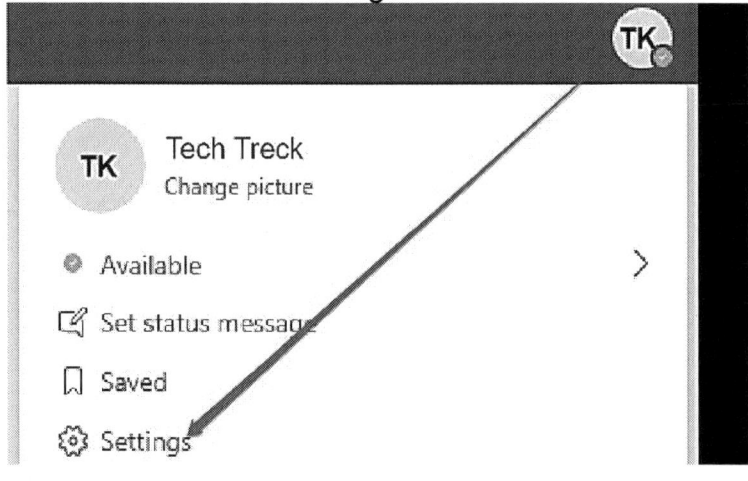

Next, you can choose **Dark** from the theme option available.

Settings

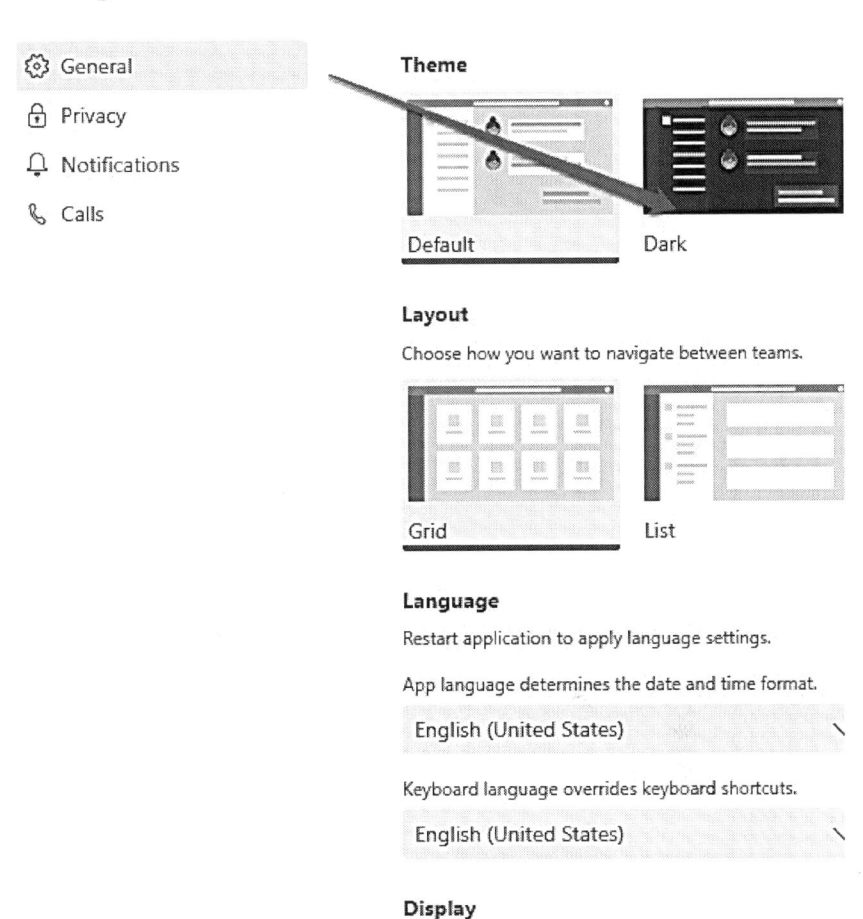

- General
- Privacy
- Notifications
- Calls

Theme

Default   Dark

Layout

Choose how you want to navigate between teams.

Grid   List

Language

Restart application to apply language settings.

App language determines the date and time format.

English (United States)

Keyboard language overrides keyboard shortcuts.

English (United States)

Display

Turn off animations (requires restarting

HOW TO TURN ON DARK THEME ON MOBILE DEVICES

On your mobile device, while in any of your Teams, click on the hamburger menu.

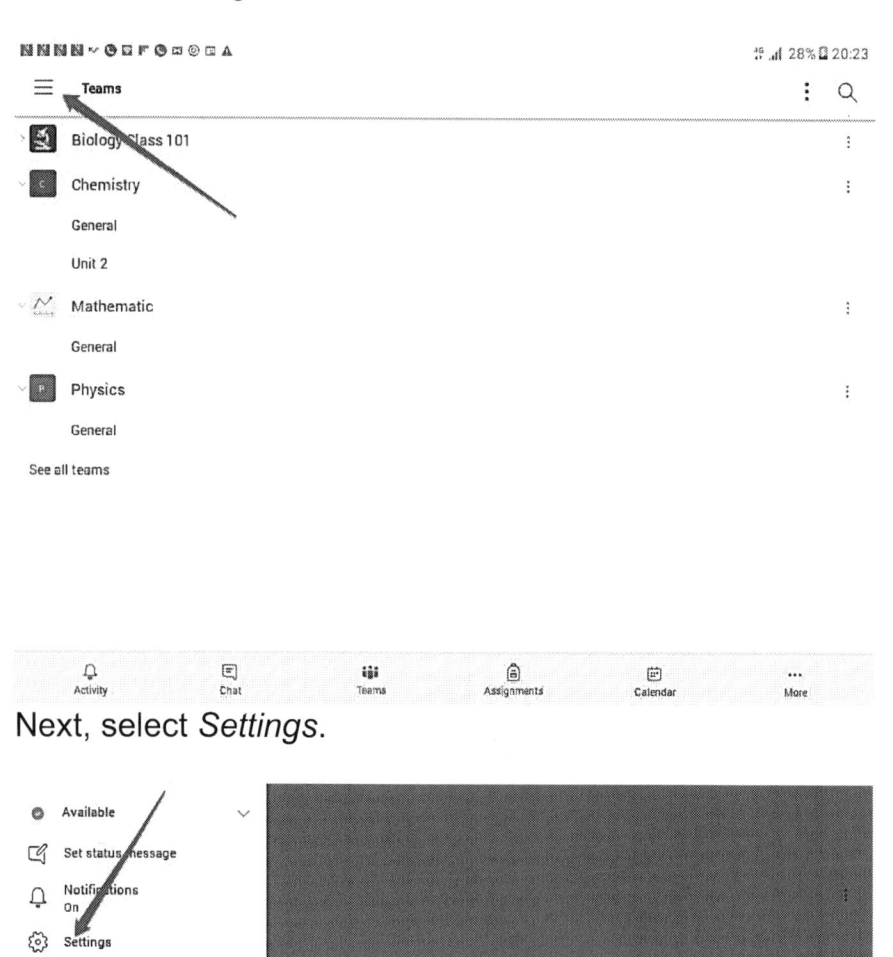

Next, select *Settings*.

You can then toggle ON Dark theme

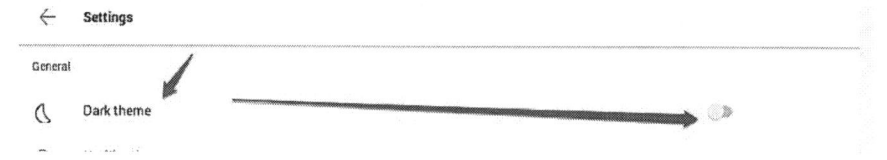

HOW TO CHANGE TEAMS LAYOUT

Click on your profile picture, then select *Settings*. Scroll down to the layout tab and make your choice.

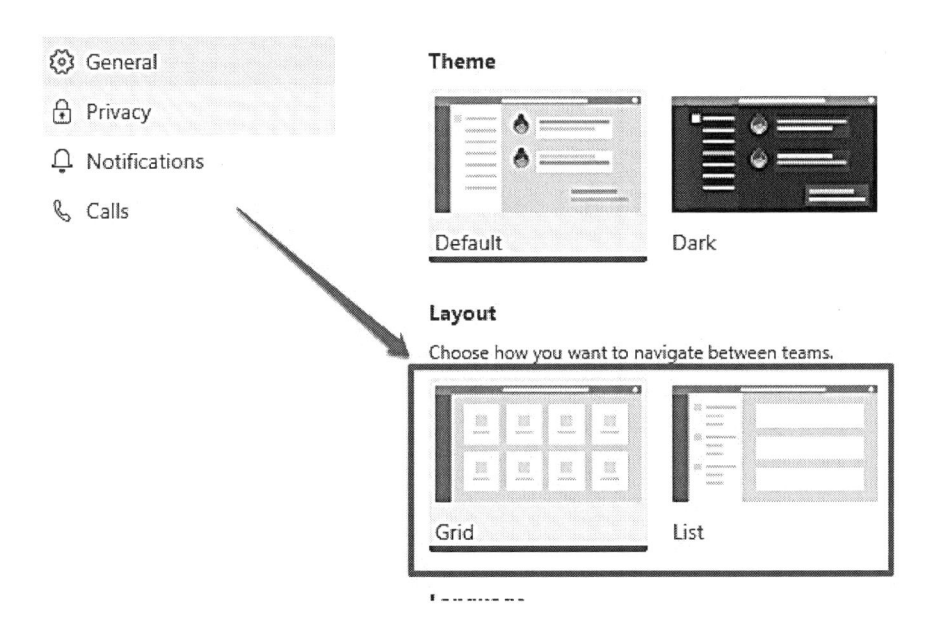

HOW TO TRANSLATE LANGUAGES IN TEAMS

Microsoft Teams now supports instant translation for messages and personal chats for over 60 supported languages.

Click on the Teams on the Navigation bar, and click on the gear icon below your profile picture.

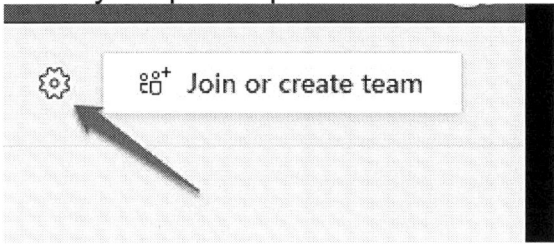

Next, select *Switch view*.

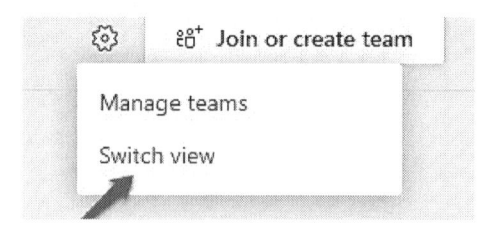

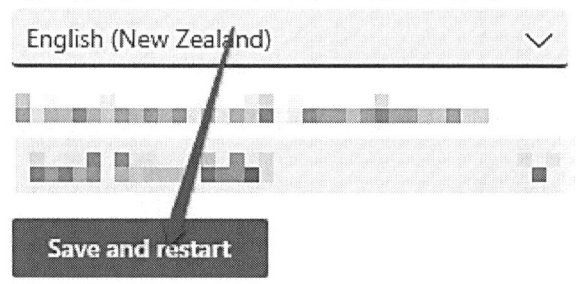

Set your language for the Teams app by clicking on the drop-down.

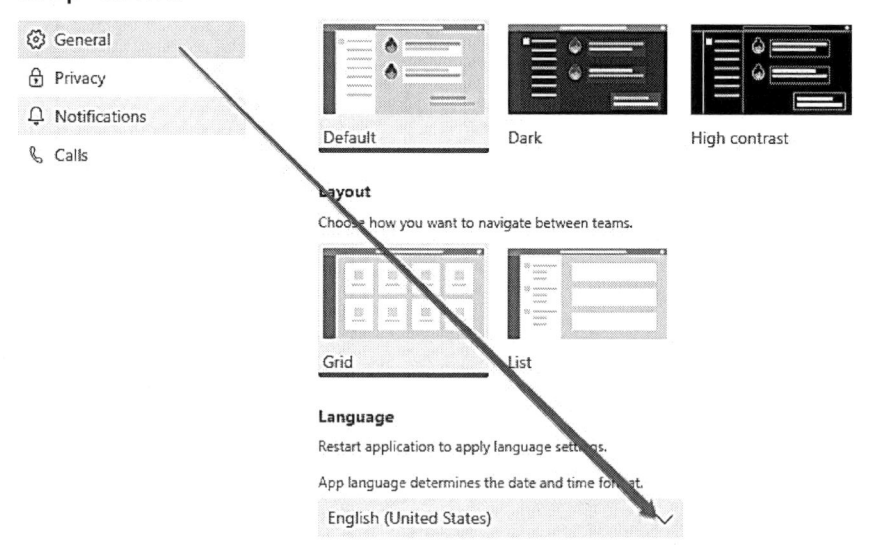

This will be the language your Teams will translate messages to when selected. Click on the Save and restart button to start using it.

During a chat, If you receive a message in another language, click on the 3-dots icon beside the chat and select *Translate* for instant translation into your chosen language for Teams.

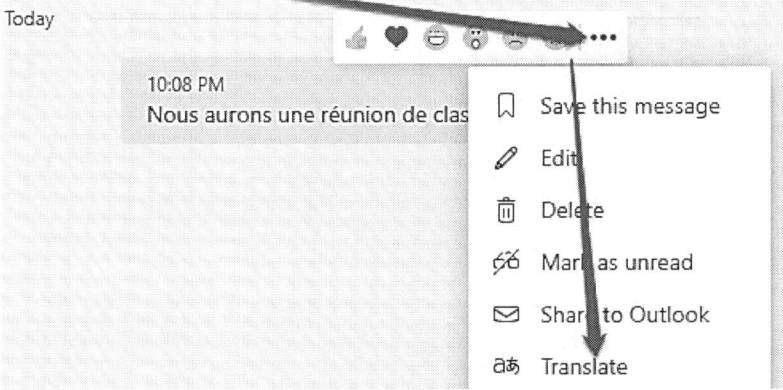

To help separate your normal Teams messages from the translated ones, Microsoft Teams will include an icon to the right of the timestamp on the content.

If you wish to undo the translation, click on the 3-dots and select *See Original Message*.

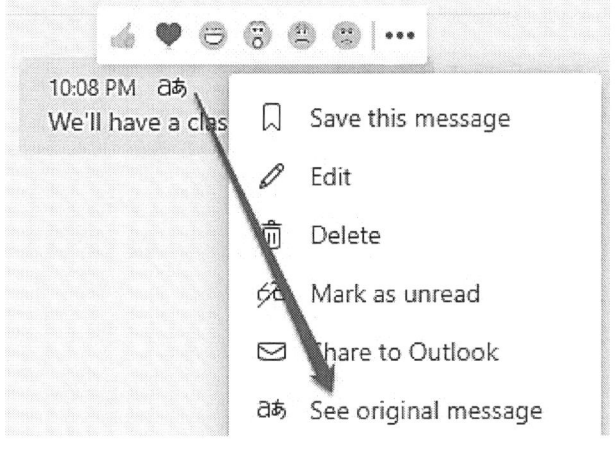

HOW TO SET KEYBOARD LANGUAGE

Click on your profile picture, and then click on *Settings*.

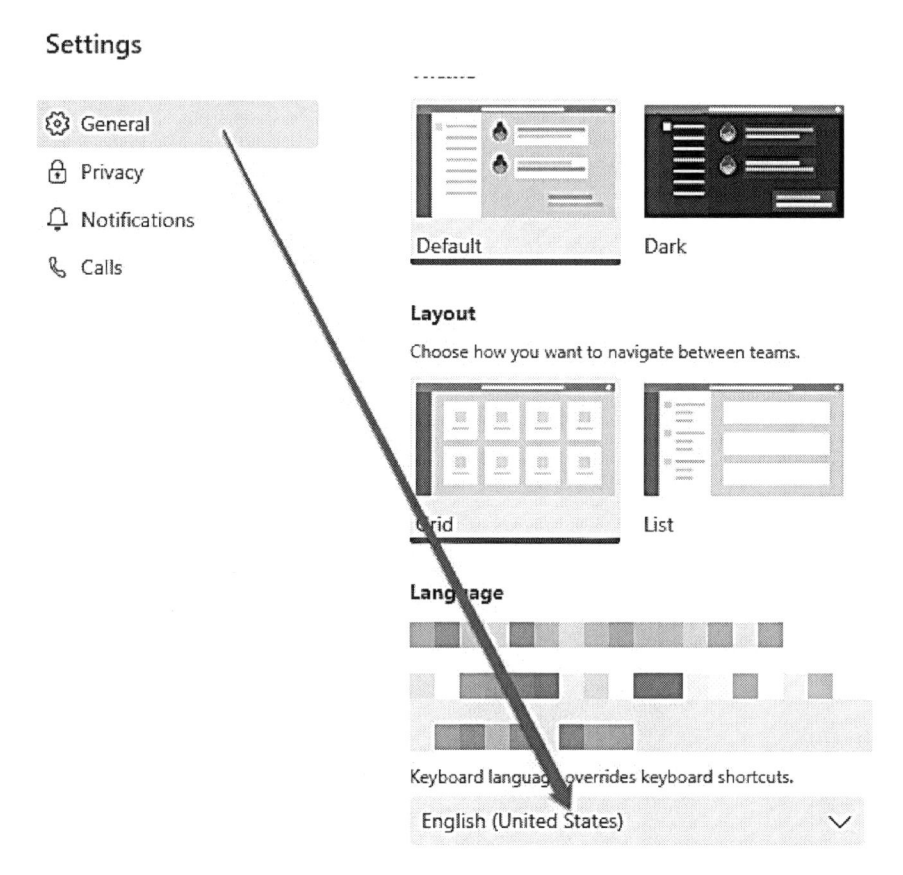

Under the General tab, go to the *Keyboard Language* section and select your preferred language.

HOW TO DISABLE TEAMS FROM STARTING AUTOMATICALLY AND RUNNING IN THE BACKGROUND WHEN CLOSED ON DESKTOPS

By default, Teams automatically opens and run in the background as soon as your device starts even when you close the app, it still runs in the background. To change this setting, click on your profile picture and select Settings.

Under the General tab, go to the Application section and disable the auto-start and on close settings.

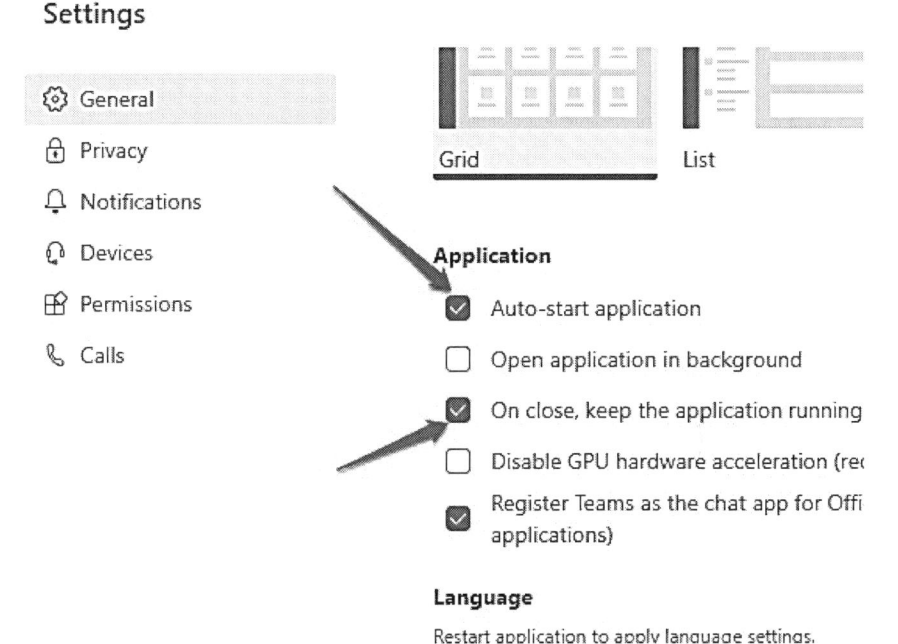

HOW TO BLOCK CALLS WITH NO CALLER ID

Click on your profile picture, click on *Settings,* and click on the Privacy tab. Locate and click on Block calls with no caller ID

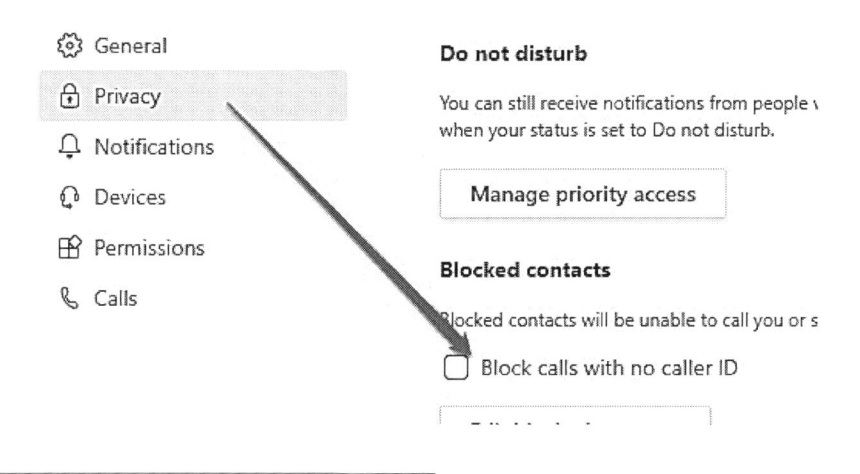

HOW TO FILTER YOUR ACTIVITY FEEDS

Filtering the activity feeds in Microsoft Teams is a way of cluttering your information. Click on the Activity tab, to locate and click on the Filter icon.

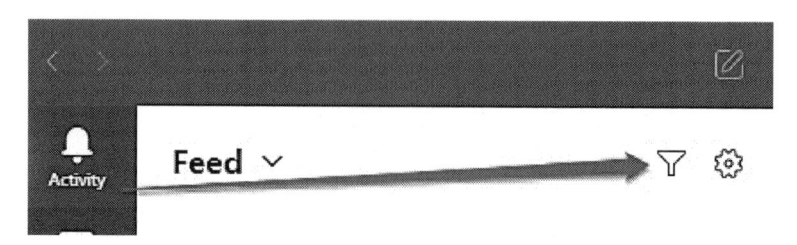

Select your setting from the list of options.

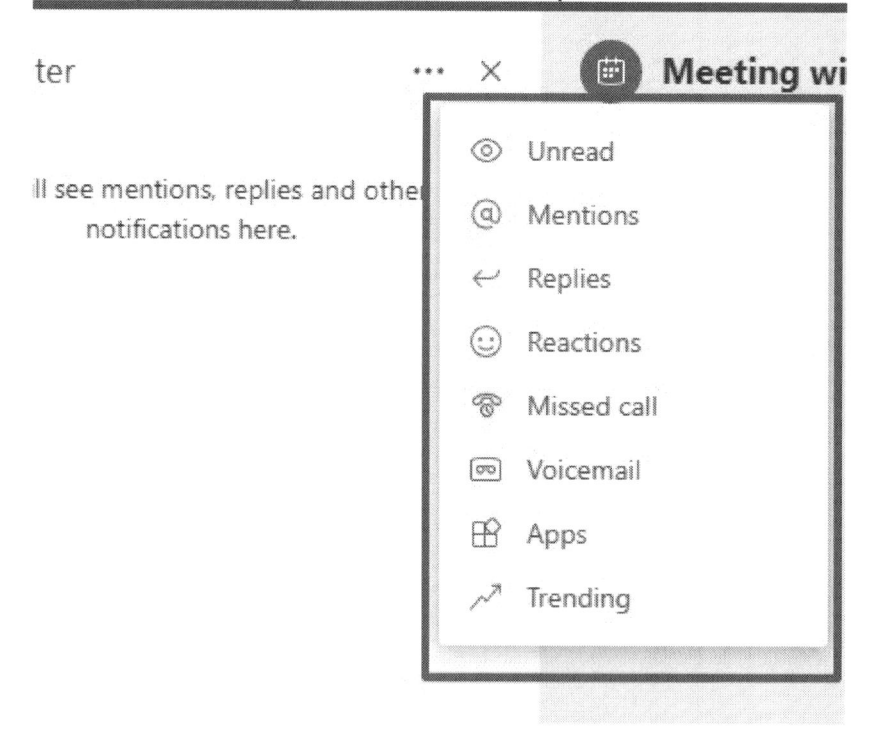

- Unread
- Mentions
- Replies
- Reactions
- Missed call
- Voicemail
- Apps
- Trending

HOW TO QUICKLY NAVIGATE, EXECUTE COMMANDS, AND SEARCH WITHIN MICROSOFT TEAMS

If you have many teams and channels that you access often, instead of using the Navigation bar to browse items manually, you can quickly navigate to them using the Microsoft Teams search bar.

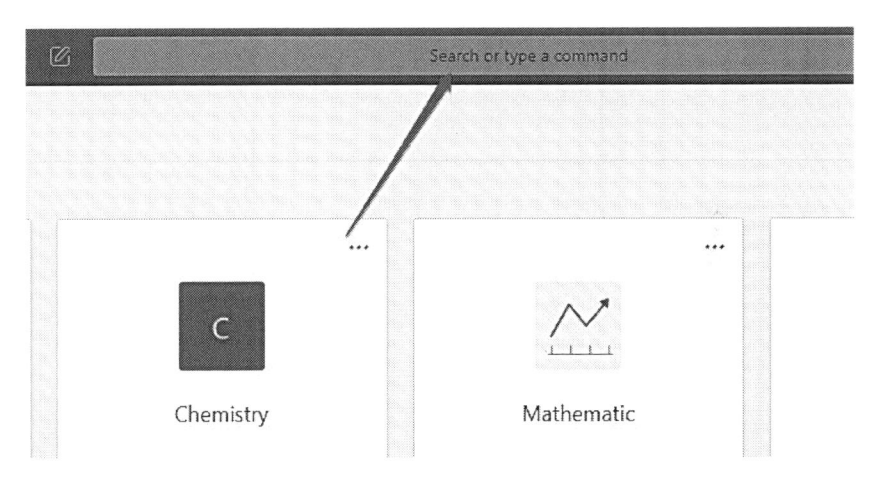

With the search bar as your navigation tool, you can navigate to several areas within Microsoft teams like; going to a Teams, Channels, and participant as well as apps like Planner or OneNote

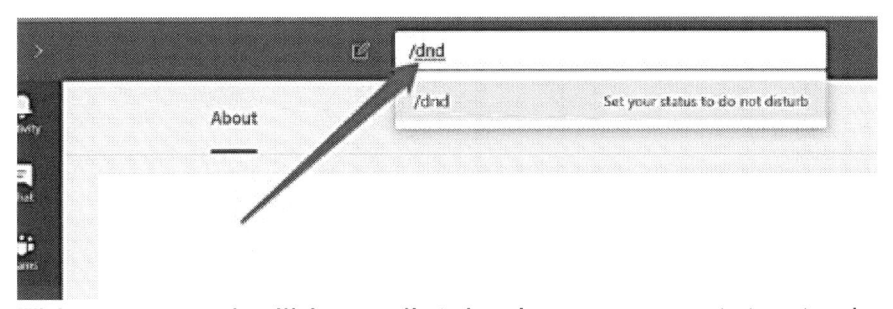

This command will immediately change your status to do not disturb.

EMAILS MESSAGE TO CHANNELS

You can use the email address of your channel to send messages. First, you have to get the email address and the go-to your google or yahoo mail to send a message directly to your channel.

To get the email address of your channel, click on the 3-dots beside the channel icon, and select Get email address.

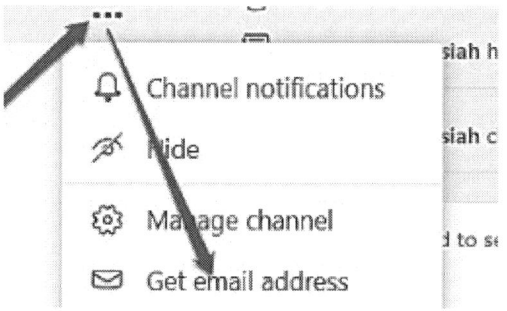

Copy and paste the address to send a mail to the channel.

MICROSOFT TEAMS KEYBOARD SHORTCUTS

Using Microsoft Teams Keyboard shortcuts increases your speed. For a quick view of essential Teams shortcuts, on your keyboard type Ctrl +.

General

Ctrl + 1	-	Open Activity
Ctrl + 2	-	Open Chat
Ctrl + N	-	Start a new chat
Ctrl + 3	-	Open Teams
Ctrl + 4	-	Open Calendar
Ctrl + 5	-	Open Calls
Ctrl + 6	-	Open Files
Ctrl + Shift + F	-	Open Filter
Ctrl + Slash (/)	-	Show commands
Ctrl + Comma (,)	-	Open Settings
F1	-	Open Help
Esc	-	Close
Ctrl + Equal Sign (=)	-	Zoom in
Ctrl + Minus Sign (-)	-	Zoom out

Meetings and calls

Ctrl + Shift + N	-	Schedule a meeting
Ctrl + S	-	Save/send a meeting request
Ctrl + Shift + C	-	Start audio call
Ctrl + Shift + S	-	Accept audio call
Ctrl + Shift + U	-	Start video call
Ctrl + Shift + A	-	Accept video call
Ctrl + Shift + D	-	Decline call
Ctrl + Shift + M	-	Toggle audio (mute/unmute)
Ctrl + Shift + O	-	Toggle video
Ctrl + Shift + F	-	Toggle fullscreen

Ctrl + Shift + P - Toggle background blur in video call

Screen sharing
Ctrl + Shift + Space - Go to sharing toolbar
Ctrl + Shift + E - Share your screen
Ctrl + Shift + A - Accept screen share
Ctrl + Shift + D - Reject screen share

Messaging
C - Go to compose box
Ctrl + Shift + X - Expand compose box
Ctrl + Enter - Send (expanded compose box)
Ctrl + Shift + X - Mark message as important
Ctrl + O - Attach file
Shift + Enter - Start new line
R - Reply to thread
Ctrl + Shift + I - Mark as important

Navigation
Ctrl + G - Go to
Ctrl + E - Go to Search
Alt + Up Arrow - Go to previous list item
Alt + Down Arrow - Go to next list item
Ctrl + Shift + Up Arrow - Move selected team up
Ctrl + Shift + Down Arrow - Move selected team down
Ctrl + Shift + F6 - Go to previous section
Ctrl + F6 - Go to next section

HOW TO SIGN OUT OF TEAMS

When you click on your profile button, you find the Sign out tab to leave the Teams.

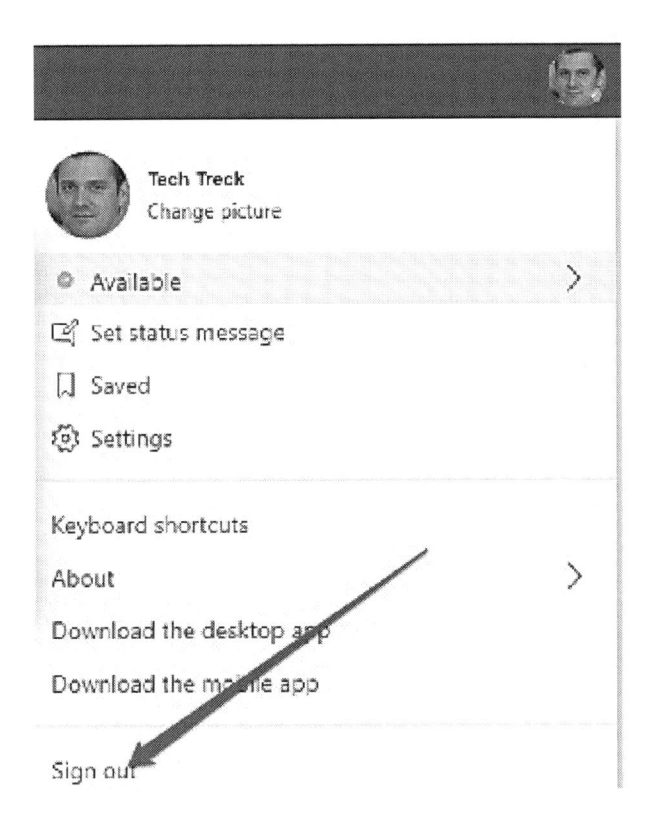

Manufactured by Amazon.ca
Bolton, ON